CHEMISTRY

LAB MANUAL

CLASS-XI

A Complete Lab Activity Book

Authors

Mr. Rohit Manglik
(NIT, Surathkal)

Mr. Kaushalesh Dwivedi
(M.Sc., B.Ed.)

Strictly according to the latest syllabus prescribed by

Central Board of Secondary Education (CBSE)

And

State Boards of Chhattisgarh, Haryana, Bihar, Jharkhand, Kerala, Mizoram,

Meghalaya, and other states following the CBSE curriculum

Title	: Chemistry Lab Manual - XI
Author Name	: Mr. Rohit Manglik, Mr. Kaushalesh Dwivedi
Published By	: EduGorilla Community Pvt. Ltd.
Publishers Address	: 12/651, First Floor Opp. Arvindo Park, Near Jama Masjid, Indira Nagar, Lucknow, Uttar Pradesh - 226016, India

Copyright

Disclaimer

Although the author and publisher have made every effort to ensure the accuracy of information in this book, we do not assume any responsibility to errors and hereby disclaim any liability to any party for any loss, damage, or disruption caused by errors or omissions, whether such errors or omissions result from negligence, accident, or any other cause.

Compiled and Created by EduGorilla Book Experts

Printed by EduGorilla Community Pvt. Ltd.

PREFACE

With the NEP 2020 and expansion of research and knowledge has changed the face of education to a great extent. In the Modern times, education is not just constricted top the lecture method but also includes a practical knowledge of certain subjects. This way of education helps a student to grasp the basic concepts and principles. Thus, trying to break the stereotype that subjects like Mathematics, and Science means studying lengthy formulas, complex structures, and handling complicated instruments, we are trying to make education easy, fun, and enjoyable.

The new CBSE syllabus for Science Practical includes content-based experiments, which help in comprehension of concepts and try to develop the scientific attitude and basic laboratory skills desired at this level.

The present book Chemistry Lab Manual Class XI has been written to meet the requirements of new curriculum in the practical work for class 11 following NEP 2020.

The purpose of this manual is not only to convey the approach of the laboratory courses but also to provide the students appropriate guidance required for carrying out the experiments in science laboratories. All the experiments in this manual have been given to conform a systematic format that includes Aim, Theory, Material Required, Procedure, Observation, Result, Precautions, Viva-Voce and Suggested Activities.

The Theory given with each experiment is a very special feature of this lab manual. It gives the complete understanding of each Concept/Term & Definition etc. so that students need not to refer their textbooks or any other book. Viva-Voce questions given with each experiment aims to test a student's understanding of the related experiment. To provide the student a basic idea of investigatory projects, some investigatory projects have been included as well.

SOME SPECIAL FEATURES

- Detailed and step-by-step procedure for each experiment.
- Viva-voce questions been designed to have grasp on the skill & knowledge required for an experiment
- Clearly labelled diagrams demonstrate the correct way of handling laboratory apparatus and pert the experiments methodically.

SYLLABUS

Time Allowed: 3 Hours   **Max. Marks: 30**

Evaluation Scheme for Examination	Marks
• Volumetric Analysis	08
• Salt Analysis	08
• Content Based Experiment	06
• Project work	04
• Class Record and Viva	04
Total	30

PRACTICAL SYLLABUS

Total Periods: 60

**Micro-chemical methods are available for several of the practical experiments.
Wherever possible, such techniques should be used.**

A. Basic Laboratory Techniques
1. Cutting glass tube and glass rod
2. Bending a glass tube
3. Drawing out a glass jet
4. Boring a cork

B. Characterization and Purification of Chemical Substances
1. Determination of melting point of an organic compound
2. Determination of boiling point of an organic compound
3. Crystallization of impure sample of any one of the following: Alum, Copper sulphate, Benzoic acid

C. Experiments based on pH
a) Any one of the following experiments:
- Determination of pH of some solutions obtained from fruit juices, solution of known and varied concentrations of acids, bases and salts using pH paper or universal indicator.
- Comparing the pH of solutions of strong and weak acids of same concentration.
- Study the pH change in the titration of a strong base using universal indicator.

b) Study the pH change by common ion in case of weak acids and weak bases.

D. Chemical Equilibrium
One of the following experiments:
a) Study the shift in equilibrium between ferric ions and thiocyanate ions by increasing/decreasing the concentration of either of the ions.
b) Study the shift in equilibrium between $[Co(H_2O)_6]^{2+}$ and chloride ions by changing the concentration of either of the ions.

E. Quantitative Estimation
 i. Oxalic Using a chemical balance.
 ii. Preparation of standard solution of Oxalic acid.
iii. Determination of strength of a given solution of Sodium Hydroxide by titrating it against standard solution of Oxalic acid.
 iv. Preparation of standard solution of Sodium Carbonate.

v. Determination of strength of a given solution of Hydrochloric acid by titrating it against standard Sodium Carbonate solution.

F. Qualitative analysis

a) Determination of one anion and one cation in a given salt
Cations: $Pb^{2+}, Cu^{2+}, Al^{3+}, Fe^{3+}, Mn^{2+}, Ni^{2+}, Zn^{2+}, Co^{2+}, Ca^{2+}, Sr^{2+}, Ba^{2+}, Mg^{2+}, NH_4^+$
Anions: $CO_3^{2-}, S^{2-}, SO_3^{2-}, SO_4^{2-}, NO_3^-, Cl^-, Br^-, I^-, PO_4^{3-}, C_2O_4^{2-}, CH_3COO^-$
(Note: Insoluble salts excluded)
b) Detection of Nitrogen, Sulphur, Chlorine in organic compounds.

<u>PROJECT</u>

Scientific investigations involving laboratory testing and collecting information from other sources.

A few suggested Projects

- Checking the bacterial contamination in drinking water by testing sulphide ion
- Study of the methods of purification of water
- Testing the hardness, presence of Iron, Fluoride, Chloride, etc. depending upon the regional variation in drinking water and study of causes of presence of these ions above permissible limit (if any)
- Investigation of the foaming capacity of different washing soaps and the effect of addition of sodium carbonate on it.
- Study the acidity of different samples of tea leaves
- Determination of the rate of evaporation of different liquids
- Study the effect of acids and bases on the tensile strength of fibers
- Study of acidity of fruit and vegetable juices.

Note: Any other investigatory project, which involves about 10 periods of work, can be chosen with the approval of the teacher.

CONTENTS

Experiments

$$\begin{vmatrix} COOH \\ | \\ COOH \end{vmatrix} . x H_2 O$$, 6 g of which has been dissolved to make 1 L of solution. You are provided with

M/10 NaOH solution.
- Viva Voce.

(a) Determination of one cation and one anion in a given salt.
- Viva Voce.
(b) Detection of nitrogen, sulphur, chlorine, bromine and iodine in an organic compound.
- Viva Voce.

Projects

- Test the presence of ionic contamination in different samples of contaminated water.
- Checking the bacterial contamination in drinking water by testing sulphide ions.
- Investigation of the foaming capacity of different washing soaps and the effect of addition of sodium carbonate on them.
- Determination of the rate of evaporation of different liquids.
- To study the effect of acids and bases on the tensile strength of fibers.
- To study the methods of purification of water.
- To analyses the hardness of different samples of water.
- Compare the water-soluble polyphenol (catechin) content in various stamp of tea leaves.

<u>INTRODUCTION TO CBSE CLASS 11 CHEMISTRY LAB MANUAL</u>

Chemistry is an experimental science; the concepts learned in the theory classes are better understood through experimentation. Laboratory work provide an opportunity to observe many of the chemical phenomena under controlled laboratory conditions and workout a problem through the method of inquiry. In other words, it provides you with ample opportunity to become a keen observe and to draw inferences and explain results.

The training in laboratory work helps to develop skills for handling apparatus and equipment and carry out experiments. In this way, the experimental work helps to promote scientific temper and adopt a cooperative attitude. Working in the laboratory provides a platform for trying novel and creative ideas and giving them concrete shape.
Chemistry is full of surprises and investigation of various chemical activities occurring around us. A systematic lab work is necessary to be done to get the correct results. The concept learned in the theory classes are better understood through experimentation. Laboratory work provides an opportunity to observe various chemical phenomena under controlled laboratory conditions and to draw inferences and explain results.

Chemistry has made a profound impact on the society. It is intimately linked to the wellbeing of all creations. The essence and understanding of the subject lie in experimentation and development of practical skills. All the theories and laws are the results of experimentation and observations made by great scientists. Also, there are many budding scientists amongst today's student community. Hence it is important that the concept of precise measurements, scientific temperament, practical skills and most importantly precautions to be taken while performing experiments must be imparted to them. Scientists learn much by discussion. In the same manner, you too may be benefitted by discussion with your teacher and classmates. Use books in case of any doubt because books are more reliable, complete and better source of information than classmates. Else consult your teacher. In order to become proficient in basic principles underlying the laboratory work, you must learn to handle the equipment and familiarise yourself with the safety measures and good laboratory practices.

You should organise yourself before entering into the laboratory for work and be aware of the pre-laboratory preparation and experimental procedures so that your work is not haphazard. You should work individually unless the experiments require teamwork.

CHEMISTRY LABORATORY

A chemistry laboratory is a workshop for chemists. Here students learn the techniques of the preparation, identification and estimation of chemical substances. Before starting experiment, a student must know from where to get the apparatus required for the given experiment and the placement of the chemicals to be used. A student must know the proper use of each equipment and the precautions to be observed while working in the laboratory. A chemistry laboratory is provided with the following fittings with which the student must become familiar.

1. **DEMONSTRATION TABLE**

   Before starting experiment, the teacher gives instructions and demonstrates the concerned experiment on demonstration table. In chemistry laboratory, no seats are made available to the students, so students stand around demonstration table and note the instructions from teacher.

2. **STUDENTS' WORKING TABLE**

   A number of wooden or concrete tables are provided for working. Each seat is provided with:

a) **REAGENT SHELVES**

   Reagents or chemicals to be used are placed on the reagent shelf. These are the reagents which are commonly used. For example, all dilute and concentrated acids such as H_2SO_4, HCl, HNO_3, etc. and bases like $NaOH$, NH_4OH, etc.

b) **SINKS AND WATER TAPS**

   A sink and a water tap are fitted between every two reagent shelves. On either side of the sink, usually two taps are fitted for supply of water.

c) GAS TAPS

These taps are fitted on the seats for supply of petrol gas to the Burners. Sometimes kerosene is used for producing gas in place of petrol.

3. SIDE SHELVES

Mostly there are two big shelves fitted on the walls of the laboratory. Reagents and chemicals, which are less frequently used, are placed in these shelves. Sometimes solid chemicals are placed in a separate shelf.

4. FUME CUP-BOARD

There is at least one fume cup-board in the comer of the laboratory. All experiments giving out poisonous gases or vapors are performed in this cup-board.

5. BALANCE ROOM

It is a small room attached to each laboratory. Here, a number of balances are kept for weighing the substances.

6. EXHAUST FANS

Two exhaust fans are provided at the two corners of the laboratory for the removal of the poisonous gases and vapors from the laboratory.

COMMON LABORATORY APPARATUS

1. SAFETY GOGGLES

One must wear safety goggles in the chemistry lab. It protects the eyes from irritation that may arise from any chemical or fumes coming out during the experiment. In case of any accidental splashing of chemicals or acids, it also protects us from the blindness of the eyes.

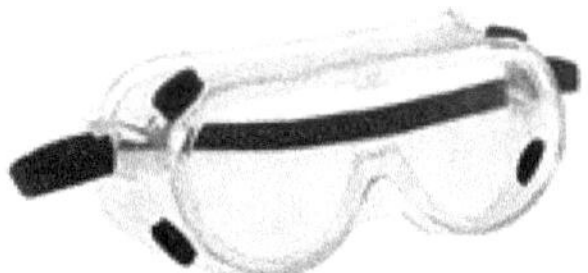

2. LAB APRON

Lab apron has a similar role as the safety goggles, but here the difference just being that instead of protecting just the eyes, it is used prevention of any injury in case of spills or splashes. for prevention of any injury in case of spills or splashes.

3. LATEX GLOVES

These gloves are useful in handling chemicals, acids, or any solutions to prevent direct contact from these chemicals with the bare hand sand skin.

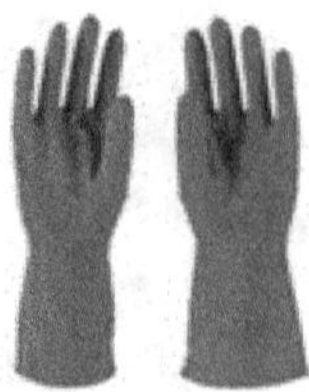

4. BEAKERS

Beakers are cylindrical utensils made up of borosilicate glass, with a flat bottom and the upper opening having a rim around it along with a spout. The spout on their rim's aids in the proper pouring of solutions and they do not have any covering on the top. Most of the time watch glasses are used to cover their solutions. They are of varying sizes and are used to hold, heat, or mix substances with a proper measure. Although they come with graduated calibrations, they are not meant for precise calculations of solutions, and as such other apparatus come handy in this.

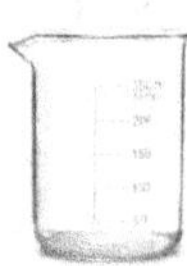

5. TEST TUBES

The next very common apparatus are the test tubes. They are usually cylindrical pipes made up of glass, with a circular opening on one side and a rounded bottom on the other. They come in different sizes but the most common standard size is 18*150 mm. Test tubes are one of the most important apparatuses as they are functional from storing to mixing reagents in any chemical or biological reactions. They become very handy when a large number of samples need to be tested for qualitative assessment of any test.

6. CONICAL FLASKS

Conical flask, also known as Erlenmeyer flask, is an apparatus having a flat bottom and a long narrow neck, which allows easy mixing of the solution without spilling out the content. Since the flask has a narrow long neck, it is also used to gently heat the content inside with a gentle swirling motion of the flask. The flask can also be covered using a rubber cap or cork. One should always remember never to heat any flask with its cap on as it will lead to pressure and gas build up inside the closed flask and lead to explosion.

7. BOILING FLASK

Boiling flasks, also known as Florence flask, has a round bottom with a long neck. It can be capped using rubber or glass stoppers and is mostly used to hold solutions that can be easily heated with proper swirling motions for proper mixing.

8. VOLUMETRIC FLASKS

This is one of the most important glassware of any lab, which is made up of glass and is calibrated to hold a precise volume of liquids at any precise temperature. Different sizes of volumetric flasks are available, each calibrated for exact measurement of liquids and solutions. It is mostly used in the preparation of standard solution.

9. DROPPERS

The dropper, also known as Pasteur pipette, is a common small apparatus, usually made up of plastic or glass cylinder, having a small nozzle on one side and a rubber holder on the other. It is used to put the liquids or solutions in any medium dropwise, that is, one drop at a time, necessary equipment when any reagent is required in an extremely small amount in a solution.

10. PIPETTES

Pipettes are of varying sizes, designed for accomplishing specific goals of volumes. These are narrow glass cylindrical pipes, used for measuring an exact volume of liquid and placing it into another container.

11. CRUCIBLE

Crucibles are made up of porcelain and are used to store and heat substances when required to be heated at high temperatures since glassware are not always suitable for such high heat involving experiments.

12. FUNNELS

Funnels are necessary equipment to pour substances and solutions in narrow-mouthed test tubes and conical flasks. There is variety of its available, most common ones are filter, thistle, and dropping funnels.

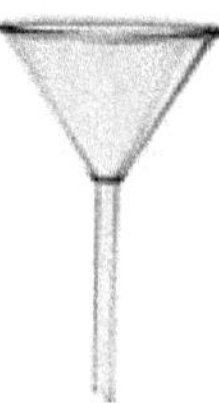

13. BRUSHES

Brushes serve as the cleansing apparatus of the test tubes, as they are the only things that can get fit into the narrow-mouthed test tubes and other cylindrical and narrow objects.

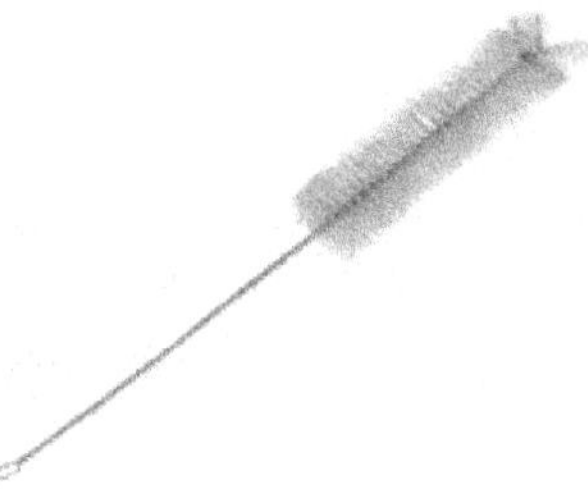

14. WATCH GLASS

This apparatus is more commonly found in chemistry laboratories and is made up of a concave piece of glass. It is normally used to hold solids, evaporate liquids, and heat small quantities of different substances as per the need of the experiment.

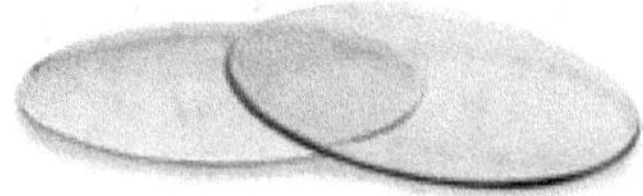

15. BURETTE

It's mostly used in the titration reactions, and is handful in delivering a known volume of any substance to other equipment. This apparatus is a long-graduated tube, with a stopcock present at the lower end. It usually comes in the sizes of 10ml, 25ml or 50ml.

INSTRUCTIONS TO WORK IN LABORATORY

To work in the laboratory, a student must follow the following rules:

1. A student must have a practical notebook, rough note-book for instructions, a pen or pencil, a laboratory coat and other equipment such as a platinum wire, fractional weights as required.
2. Always come prepared for the experiment. This will help in understanding the experiment better.
3. Always listen to the teacher's instructions carefully and note down the important points and precautions to be followed.
4. After the instructions, collect the apparatus from the laboratory assistant in queue.
5. Thoroughly clean the apparatus to be used.
6. Do only the experiments assigned, unallotted experiments should not be done.
7. Do your experiment honestly without caring for the final result. Record the observations on a rough note-book instead of writing on the pieces of paper.
8. Plan your work so that it is finished in the stipulated time.
9. Be economical with the reagents. Only small quantities of the reagents are to be used.
10. Handle the glass apparatus very carefully. In case of any breakage, report it to your teacher at once.
11. Dispose of all waste liquids in the sink and allow water to run for some time by opening the water tap.
12. Keep your seat clean. If an acid or other corrosive chemical is spilled, wash it off with water.
13. Clean your apparatus after the experiment and return it to the laboratory assistant.
14. In case of any injury or accident or breakage of the apparatus, report it to the teacher immediately.
15. Wash your hands with soap after the experiment.

SOME IMPORTANT PRECAUTIONS

To avoid unnecessary risk or injury during laboratory work, the students are advised to observe the following precautions:

1. Do not touch any chemical with hand as some of them may be corrosive.
2. Never taste a chemical. It may be poisonous.
3. Do not place the chemical on the palm of your hand.
4. Do not keep the reagent bottles open.
5. Do not roam here and there in the laboratory without work.
6. Do not put any object into the reagent bottle.
7. Do not bring inflammable liquids such as alcohol, ether near the flame.
8. Do not take the reagent from the shelf to your seat.
9. Do not disturb the arrangement of reagents placed on the shelf.
10. Do not use cracked glass apparatus such as beakers for heating purposes.
11. Do not keep water tap running when not required.
12. Do not throw solid waste materials like filter paper pieces, test-tube pieces, etc. in the sink. Throw them in the waste box only.
13. Do not heat beakers or China dish directly on flame. Always make use of wire gauge.

PRACTICAL NOTE-BOOK

All the experiments that are conducted in the laboratory are recorded in a practical note-book. It is compilation of whole work done by the student, so it must be well maintained, protected from mechanical and chemical damage. For keeping up-to-date record of experiments following points should be kept in mind.

1. AIM
2. MATERIAL REQUIRED
3. THEORY
4. PROCEDURE
5. CHEMICAL REACTIONS
6. DIAGRAM
7. OBSERVATION
8. CALCULATION
9. RESULT
10. PRECAUTIONS
11. DISCUSSION

FIRST AID EMERGENCY TREATMENT IN THE LABORATORY

A chemistry laboratory encompasses different types of chemicals, apparatus. Any lack of attention on the part of student may cause accident. Accidents may occur by chance also. In any case prompt action should be taken to give first aid to the victim and then should be hospitalized if the need be. The probable accidents and their first aid emergency treatment are given below:

Types of accidents	First aid emergency treatment
1. Burns: (i) Burn by dry heat (i.e., flame, hot object etc.) (ii) Burns causing blisters. Caution. Heat burns should never be washed. (iii) Acid burns (iv) Bromine burns	(i) Apply Burner or Sarson (mustard) oil. (ii) Apply Burner at once. (iii) Wash freely with water, then with 1 Sceptic acid and again with water. Dry the skin and apply Burner. (iv) Wash liberally with 2%NH_3 solution and then rub glycerine. Wipe off glycerine after some time and apply burnol.
2. Cuts: (i) Minor cuts (ii) Serious cuts	(i) Allow to bleed for a few seconds. Remove the glass piece if any. Apply a little methylated spirit and cover with a piece of cotton. Alternatively apply $FeCl_3$ solution to stop bleeding. (ii) Apply pressure above the cut to stop bleeding. Call the doctor.
3. Eye Accidents: (i) Acid in eye (ii) Alkali in eye	(i) Wash thoroughly with water, then with 1% sodium bicarbonate solution and then with water again. (ii) Wash thoroughly with water and then with 1% boric acid solution.
4. Poisons: (i) Poisons not swallowed (ii) Acid swallowed (iii) Caustic alkalis swallowed	(i) Spit out immediately. Wash mouth with water. (ii) Drink lot of water. Drink lime water. No emetic should be taken. (iii) Drink lot of water. Drink a glass of lemon or orange juice. No emetic should be taken.

(iv) Inhalation of gases like Cl_2, SO_2, Br_2 etc causing suffocation.	(iv) Loosen the clothes at the neck. Go in the open air. Inhale dilute vapors of ammonia or gargle with sodium bicarbonate solution.

5. **Fire:**
  (i) Clothes catch fire
  (ii) Beaker containing inflammable liquid catches fire
	(i) Do not run. Wrap with a blanket. Lie down on the floor and roll.
	(ii) Cover the beaker with duster or damp cloth.

Go to the doctor after getting first aid.

BASIC LABORATORY TECHNIQUES 

In the chemical laboratory a student is required to carry out from simplest operations like bending of glass tube, cutting glass tube, boring a cork, to complex process of analyzing sub-stances qualitatively and quantitatively. A general acquaintance with such operations thus becomes obvious before taking up actual experiments. As most of these processes involve heating so knowledge of using a Burner is essential.

Experiment 1

AIM

To cut a glass tube or rod of a required length and round off its edges

MATERIAL REQUIRED
Glass tube or rod, triangular file, Bunsen Burner

PROCEDURE
Cutting a glass tube is primarily required for making U-shaped tubes, delivery tubes and other purposes. Hence a student must know how-to cut-glass tube of required length for specified purpose without injuring hands.

For cutting a glass tubing, proceed in the following manner:
1. Select a glass tubing free of cracks.
2. Place it on the bench, hold it firmly and make a single deep scratch with triangular file. Do not apply too much pressure.
3. Place the thumbs on each side of the scratch at equal distances from it. Apply gentle pressure and give a quick bending motion towards you until it breaks smoothly (Fig. 2.2).
4. Sometimes, the ends of the tube are not smooth and might bruise your fingers (Figs. 2.2 and 2.3). These can be further smoothened by rotating the ends in a flame for 2-3 minutes. The edges will be smoothened (Fig. 2.3). Allow it to cool while holding in your hand.

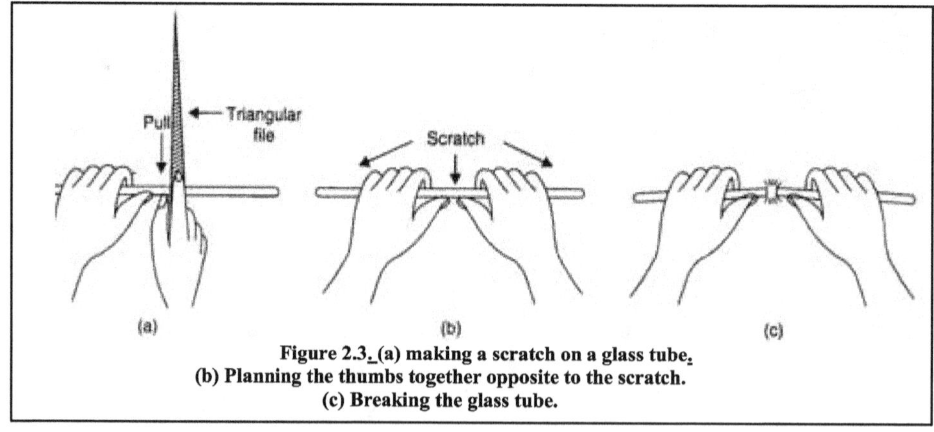

Figure 2.3. (a) making a scratch on a glass tube.
(b) Planning the thumbs together opposite to the scratch.
(c) Breaking the glass tube.

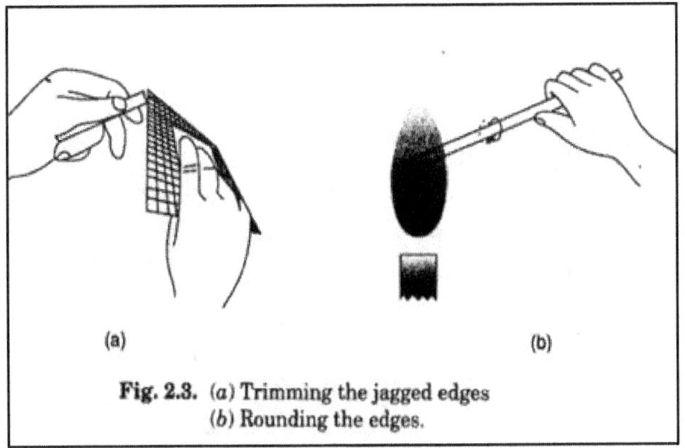

Fig. 2.3. (*a*) Trimming the jagged edges
(*b*) Rounding the edges.

PRECAUTION

1. Make a single deep scratch at the desired length with one stroke of the file.
2. To avoid injury, hold the glass tube with the help of a thick piece of cloth.
3. Do not heat the end for long time. It may seal the end or make it narrower.

AIM
To bend a glass tube at a given angle

MATERIAL REQUIRED
Glass tubing, Bunsen Burner, asbestos

PROCEDURE
For bending a glass tube proceed as follows:

1. Hold the glass tubing between the thumb and fingers, introduce it lengthwise in the luminous flame of Burner. Keep the tube rotating till it softens.

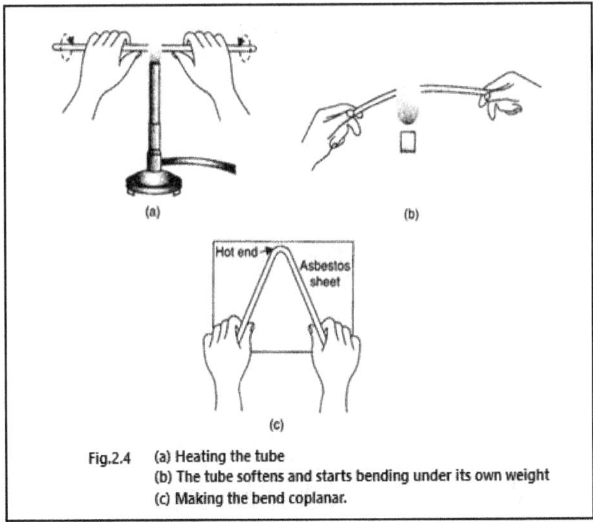

Fig.2.4   (a) Heating the tube
(b) The tube softens and starts bending under its own weight
(c) Making the bend coplanar.

2. Now apply gentle pressure so that it bends by its own weight. When the desired angle is formed, remove the tubing from the flame.

3. Place the bent limb on the asbestos sheet. Press it gently so as to make it coplanar. Allow the tubing to cool.

PRECAUTION
1. Select a glass tube of sufficient length to keep your hands safe from heat. Do not try to bend very small glass tubes of the lengths less than 20 cm.
2. While heating, the glass tube should be rotated in order to ensure uniform heating.
3. Never bend the glass tubing by force. By doing so, the tubing may break.

AIM
To draw a jet

MATERIAL REQUIRED
Glass tubing, Bunsen Burner.

PROCEDURE
1. Take a delivery tube of required length and diameter. Hold it with both hands and place it lengthwise in flame (Fig. 2.5).
2. Keep rotating the tube so as to ensure uniform heating, continue heating till it softens.
3. Take the tubing out of the flame and gently pull the two ends apart. The middle portion is drawn out to a thickness of about 2 mm.
4. Cool and cut the narrow portion with a triangular file and two jets will be obtained. Finally round the ends of the jets by heating in a flame for a short while.

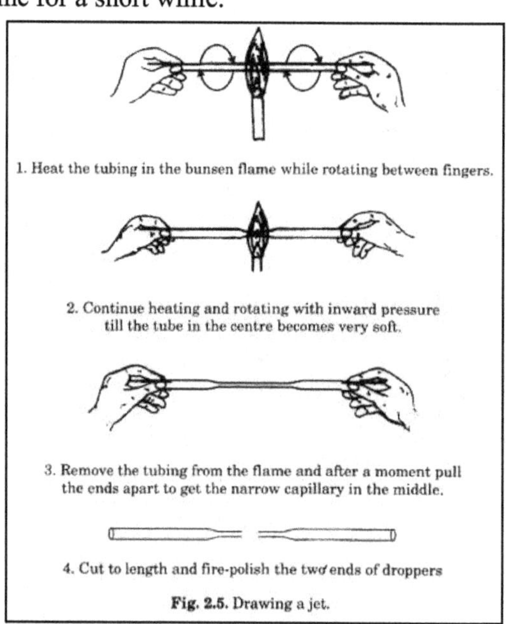

Fig. 2.5. Drawing a jet.

PRECAUTION
While drawing a jet, pull apart the two ends of the red-hot tube slowly so that it becomes thin uniformly.

Experiment 4

AIM
To bore a hole in the cork.

MATERIAL REQUIRED
A cork, Cork borer, glass tubing, cork pressure, if available

PROCEDURE
Boring a cork is required for setting up an apparatus for the preparation of gas and for carrying / out distillation etc. Above all, it is required for fitting up a wash bottle. For perfect boring of the cork, the following steps are involved:

1. **SOFTENING OF THE CORK**

   It is essential as a cork gets hard on keeping. In order to soften a cork, wet it with water. When it becomes more flexible and does not crack readily, then press it in a cork-presser which is a mechanical device and if it is not available, simply press the wetted cork under your shoes after wrapping the cork in a piece of paper.

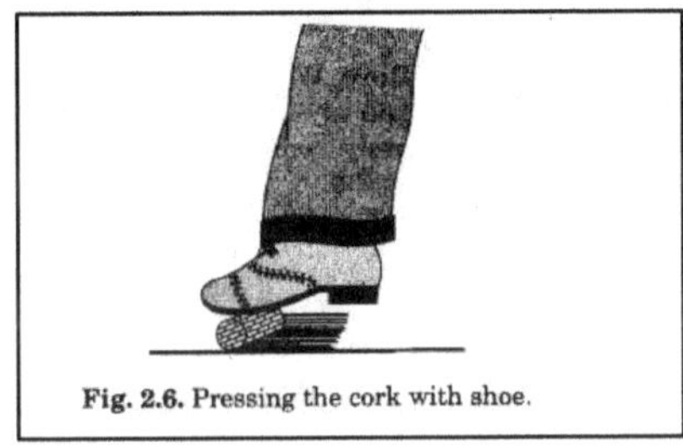

Fig. 2.6. Pressing the cork with shoe.

2. **SELECTION OF THE BORER**

   Choose a borer slightly smaller in diameter than that of the tube to be fitted in the cork. This will ensure tight fitting of the tube.

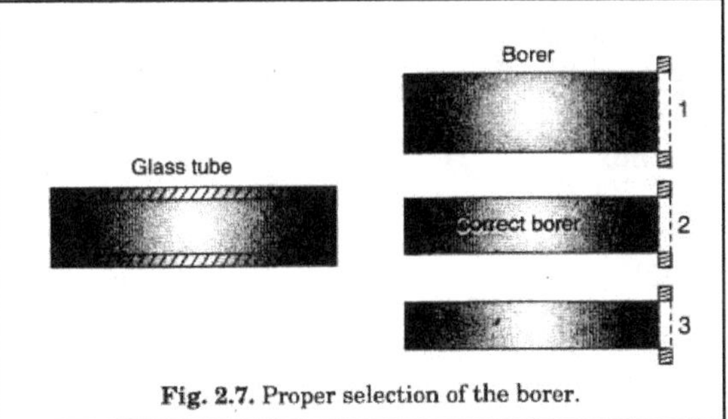

Fig. 2.7. Proper selection of the borer.

3. **BORING OF THE CORK**

   Place the cork on the table with its narrow end upward. Mark the position of the borer on both the sides of the cork to ensure straight hole. Holding the cork 'tightly with left hand, apply force on the border with a twisting motion. Apply some glycerin to the borer if it is a rubber cork. Glycerin acts as lubricant for the hard rubber cork. When half of the cork has been bored, take the borer out and reverse the cork. Start the process of boring taking care that the borer remains vertical throughout. Remove the borer after the cork has been bored from one face to the other. Remove the pieces of the cork inside by inserting the needle.

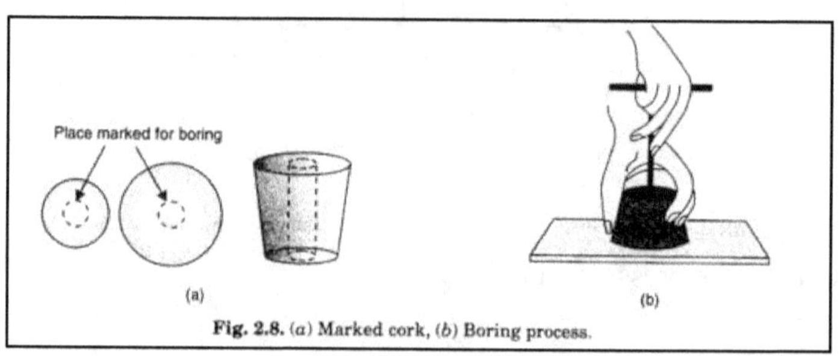

Fig. 2.8. (*a*) Marked cork, (*b*) Boring process.

> *Note:*
> *For fitting up a wash bottle, it is necessary to bore two holes in the cork. The two holes are bored in the same way as done for single hole but with a precaution that the two holes should not be very close to each other. If the distance is very small, then the thin cork layer may break.*

4. FITTING THE GLASS TUBE IN THE BORE

Wet the cork with water. Wet the end of the tube also with water. Hold the cork in one hand say left hand and tube in the right hand. It should be noted that the tube should be held closely from the wetted end. Insert the tube into the bore giving a rotatory motion as shown in Fig. 2.9.

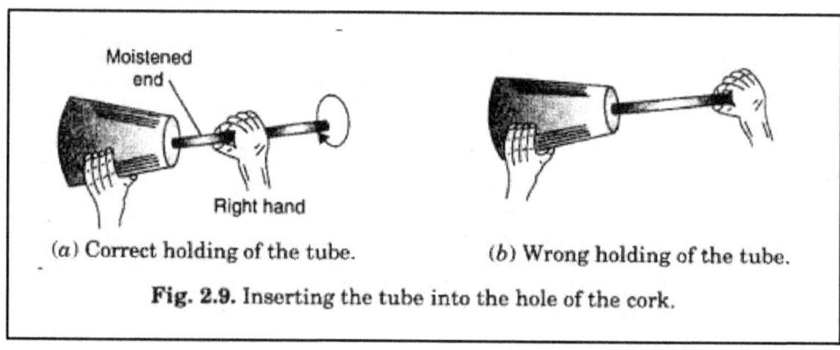

(*a*) Correct holding of the tube.   (*b*) Wrong holding of the tube.

Fig. 2.9. Inserting the tube into the hole of the cork.

PRECAUTION

1. Select bores of diameter slightly smaller in size than that of the tube to be inserted in the hole.
2. Make a mark on both sides of the cork.
3. To obtain a smooth hole, drill half the hole from one side and another half from the other side of the cork.
4. Since the rubber is hard, the end of the tube' to be inserted is usually dipped in caustic soda solution or glycerin before fitting in the hole.

Question.1. Why is a broad flame used for bending a glass tube?
Answer. If a narrow flame is used, folds are formed at the bend.

Question.2. Why does glass not possess a sharp melting point?
Answer. Glass is an amorphous solid. It does not have a regular arrangement of constituent particles. Hence, it does not have a sharp melting point.

Question.3. Which type of glass softens readily, soda lime glass or borosilicate glass?
Answer. Soda lime glass.

Question.4. Why is it required to round off the freshly cut edges of glass tube?
Answer. Freshly cut edges of glass tube are sharp. They might injure fingers while handling.

Question.5. Why should the tube be rotated while heating?

Answer. The tube is rotated while heating in order to ensure uniform heating from all sides.

Question.6. Why is the red-hot tube bent slowly?
Answer. Red hot tube is very soft. It might flatten if it is bent suddenly. Slow process of bending prevents flattening of glass tube.

Question.7. What is the role of glycerin in the process of boring?
Answer. Glycerin is used to lubricate the borer. This gives a smooth hole on boring.

Question.8. Why should the diameter of the borer be less than the diameter of the tube to be inserted in the hole?
Answer. This is done to ensure that the tube fits tightly in the hole.

Question.9. What type of glass is preferred for drawing out a jet?
Answer. Soda lime glass (soft glass) is used for drawing out a jet because it has lower melting point and hence softens easily.

CHARACTERISATION AND PURIFICATION OF CHEMICAL SUBSTANCES

DETERMINATION OF MELTING POINT

The melting point of a substance may be defined as the temperature at which the substance changes from the solid state to the liquid state. It is a very useful physical constant because a pure substance melts at a definite temperature and has a sharp melting point while an impure substance has a lower melting point and melts over a wide range. Therefore, determination of melting point is a very convenient method to check the purity of a solid substance. Moreover, melting point determination can be used to identify a substance by comparing its melting point with the melting points of known substances.

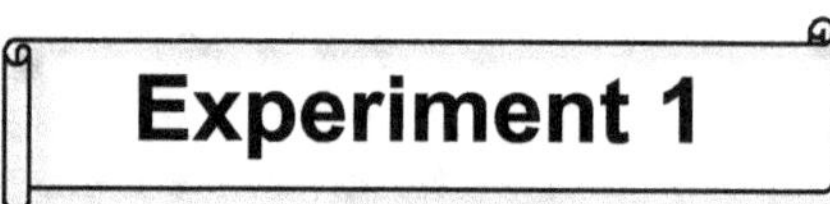

Aim

To determine the melting point of the given substance.

MATERIAL REQUIRED

Thermometer, 100 ml or 150 ml beaker, tripod stand, stirrer, iron stand, wire gauze, capillary tube 8 to 10 cm long and 1 to 2 mm diameter, spatula

PROCEDURE

1. Powder the crystalline substance. Take a capillary tube and seal its one end by heating (Fig. 3.1). For filling the substance make a heap of the powdered substance on the porous plate. Push the open end of the capillary tube into the heap. Some substance will enter into it. Now tap the sealed end of the capillary tube on the porous plate gently. Fill the capillary tube up to 2-3 mm.

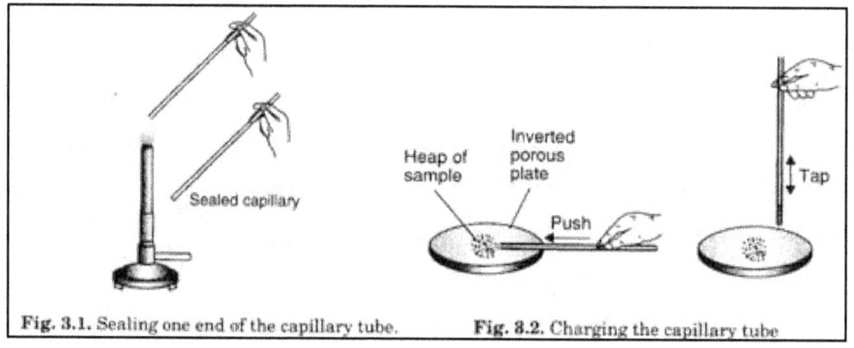

Fig. 3.1. Sealing one end of the capillary tube.   **Fig. 3.2.** Charging the capillary tube

2. Attach the capillary tube to a thermometer which is immersed in a bath of liquid paraffin. The surface tension of the bath liquid is sufficient to hold the capillary tube in position.

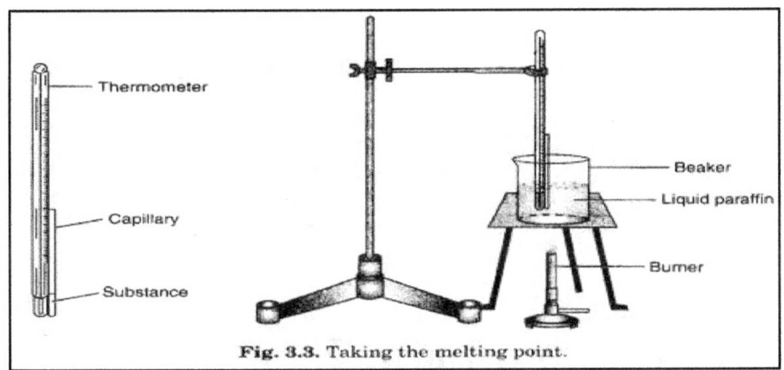

Fig. 3.3. Taking the melting point.

3. Heat the beaker slowly and go on stirring the liquid in the beaker so that the temperature remains uniform throughout. For this, a glass loop stirrer is moved up and down. When the temperature is within 15° of the melting point of the pure substance, the flame is lowered. Now, the temperature is allowed to rise slowly.
4. The temperature is noted when the substance starts melting. The temperature is noted again when it is completely melted. The average of the two readings gives the melting point of the substance.

PRECAUTIONS

1. Use dry and powdered sample for the determination of melting point.
2. Keep the lower end of the capillary tube and the thermometer at the same level.
3. Packing of the powder should be uniform without any big air gaps in between the solid particles.
4. Heating should be gradual and the bath should be stirred regularly to maintain uniform temperature.
5. The bulb of the thermometer and the capillary sticking to it should not touch the side or the bottom of the beaker.
6. Do not attach capillary tube with thermometer by a rubber band.

OBSERVATION

Temperature at which the unknown substance begins to melt = t_1°C
Temperature at which the substance completely melts = t_2°C
Melting point of the unknown substance = $(t_1+t_2^2)$ °C

Table: Melting Points of Some Organic Compounds

Compound	Melting point ($^\circ$C)	Compound	Melting point ($^\circ$C)
Phenol	42	Acetamide	82
α-Naphthol	95	Benzamide	128
β-Naphthol	123	Urea	132
Oxalic acid	101	Fructose	103
Benzoic acid	121	Glucose	146
Cinnamic acid	133	Sucrose	160
p-Toluidine	43	Naphthalene	80
α-Naphthylamine	50	Benzophenone	46

DETERMINATION OF BOILING POINT

The boiling point of a liquid may be defined as the temperature at which the vapor pressure of the liquid is equal to the atmospheric pressure exerted upon the liquid surface.

The boiling point of the liquid depends upon the pressure exerted upon the liquid surface. Since atmospheric pressure is different at different place, therefore a liquid has different boiling points at different places. For the sake of comparison, we use normal boiling points. The normal boiling point of a liquid may be defined as the temperature at which vapor pressure of the liquid is equal to one standard atmospheric pressure (760 mm).

The boiling point of a liquid increases if non-volatile impurities are present in it.

AIM

To determine the boiling point of the liquid.

MATERIAL REQUIRED

Ignition tube, thermometer, capillary tube about 6cm in length and 1-2 mm in diameter, iron stand, wire gauze, tripod stand, Burner, paraffin oil, organic liquid boiling point of which is to be determined

PROCEDURE

1. Take a small test tube and fill it two-third with the given liquid whose boiling point is to be determined. Fix this tube to the thermometer with a rubber band. The rubber band should be fixed near the mouth of the tube so that it remains outside the liquid paraffin bath. Adjust the tube so that the bottom of the tube is somewhere at the middle of the thermometer bulb.

2. Clamp the thermometer carrying test tube in an iron stand through a cork. Lower the thermometer along with the tube into a liquid paraffin bath. Adjust the thermometer so that its bulb is well under the acid and open end of the tube with the rubber band is sufficiently outside the acid bath.

3. Take a capillary tube 5-6 cm in length and seal it at about one cm from one end by heating it in flame and giving a slight twist. Place this capillary in the test tube so that sealed part of it stands in the liquid.

4. Start heating the liquid paraffin bath slowly and stir the bath gently. Keep an eye on the liquid and the test tube and also on the thread of the mercury in the thermometer. At first a bubble or two will be seen escaping at the end of the capillary dipping in the liquid, but soon a rapid and continuous stream of air bubbles escapes from it. This is the stage when the vapor pressure of the liquid in the sealed capillary just exceeds the atmospheric pressure. Note the temperature when continuous stream of bubbles starts coming out. Remove the flame and note the temperature when the evolution of bubbles from the end of, the capillary tube just stops. The mean of these two temperatures gives the boiling point of the liquid.

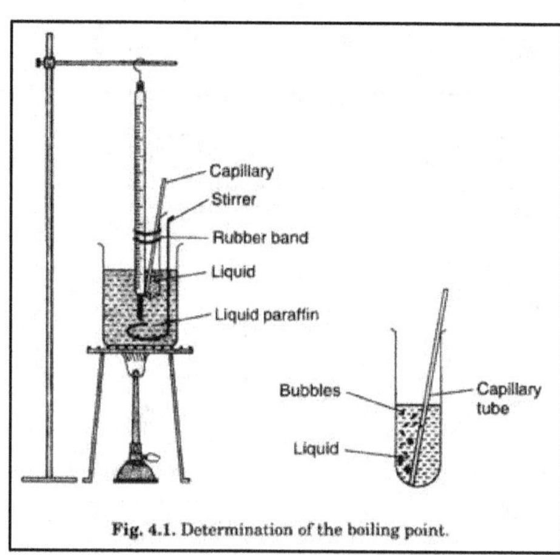

Fig. 4.1. Determination of the boiling point.

5. Allow the temperature fall by 10°C and repeat the heating and again note the boiling point.

PRECAUTIONS

1. Keep the lower end of the ignition tube and the thermometer bulb at the same level.
2. Record the temperature as the boiling point at which brisk and continuous evolution of the bubbles starts from the lower end of the capillary dipped in the liquid organic compound.
3. If on placing the sealed capillary tube in the test tube, the liquid is seen rising in the capillary tube, it indicates that the capillary tube is not properly sealed. Reject this capillary tube and use a sealed new one.
4. The sealed point of the capillary tube should be well within the liquid.

> **Note:**
> *Paraffin can be safely heated up to 220°C while conc. H_2SO_4 can be heated up to 280°C. For finding the melting points of solids, having lower melting points, liquid paraffin may be used while for solids having melting points greater than 200°C conc. H_2SO_4 may be used.*

5. The paraffin bath must be heated very slowly and the paraffin stirred to ensure uniform heating.

OBSERVATIONS

Boiling point

(i) t_1°C

(ii) t_2°C

Mean = t_1° + t_2°/2 = t°C

Table: Melting Points of Some Organic Compounds

Compound	Boiling point (°C)	Compound	Boiling point (°C)
Benzyl alcohol	205	Ethyl benzoate	212
Glycerol	290	Methyl salicylate	223
Ethylene glycol	197	Nitrobenzene	211
Phenol	182	Aniline	184
o.Cresol	190	o-Toluidine	200
Benzaldehyde	179	Chlorobenzene	132
Acetophenone	202	Bromobenzene	157
Phenyl acetate	196	Benzoyl chloride	197

PURIFICATION OF CHEMICAL SUBSTANCES BY CRYSTALLISATION

For chemical purposes the substances should be pure, completely free from any type of impurity. Impurities may be soluble or insoluble in the solvent in which the substance under consideration dissolves. So, method of purification of the substance depends on the nature of the impurity present and there are large number of methods available for the purification of the substance such as filtration, sedimentation, decantation and crystallisation. The simple laboratory technique applied for the purification of the substances by crystallisation is described below.

PROCESS OF CRYSTALLISATION

The process of crystallisation involves following steps:

1. PREPARATION OF SOLUTION OF THE IMPURE SAMPLE

I. Take a clean beaker (250 ml) and add powdered impure sample under consideration in it (~ 6.0 gm).
II. Add distilled water (25-30 ml) and stir contents gently with the help of glass rod giving circular motion as shown in Fig. 5.1.

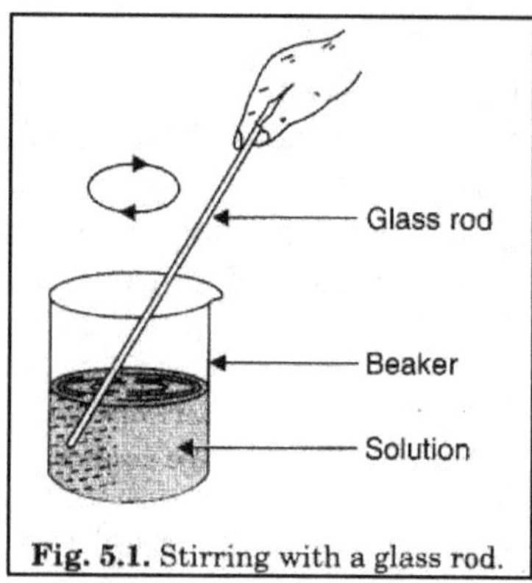
Fig. 5.1. Stirring with a glass rod.

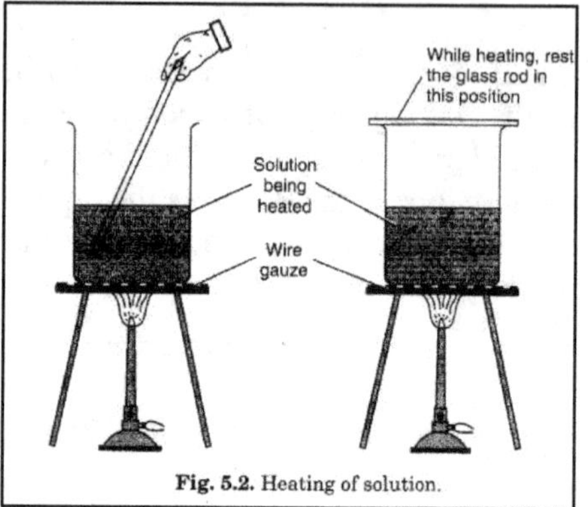

Fig. 5.2. Heating of solution.

III.   The solution in the beaker is heated (60°-70°C) on a wire gauze (Fig. 5.2).

IV.   Stir the solution continuously and add more of impure substance till no more of it dissolves.

2. FILTRATION OF HOT SOLUTION

a.   Take a circular filter paper. First fold it one-half, then fold it one-fourth as shown in Fig. 5.3. Open the filter paper, three folds on one side and one-fold on the other side to get a cone (Fig. 5.3).

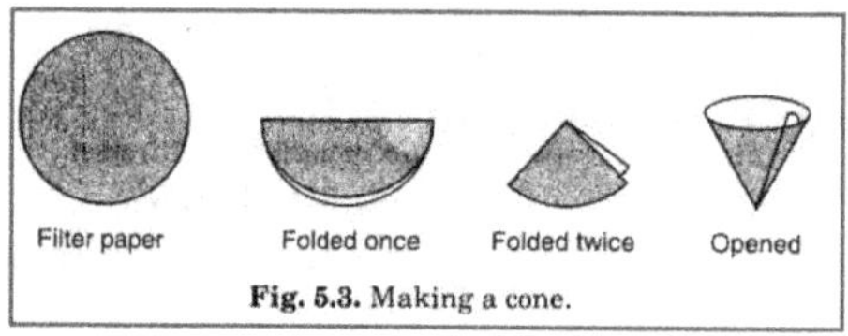

Fig. 5.3. Making a cone.

b.   Take a funnel and fit the filter paper cone into the funnel so that the upper half of the cone fits well into the funnel but lower part remains slightly away from the funnel.

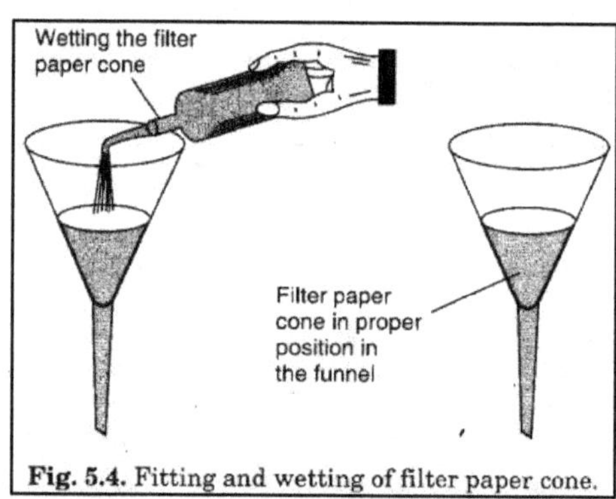

Fig. 5.4. Fitting and wetting of filter paper cone.

c.   Wet the filter paper cone with a spray of water from a wash bottle pressing the upper part of the filter paper cone gently against the wall of the funnel with the thumb (Fig. 5.4).

d.   Place the funnel on a funnel stand and place a clean China dish below the funnel for the collection of the filtrate. To avoid splashing of the filtrate, adjust the funnel so that its stem touches the wall of the dish.

e.   Hold a glass rod in slanting position in your hand or with a precaution that the lower end of the rod should reach into the filter paper cone but it does not touch it. Pour the solution along the glass rod as shown in Fig. 5.5. The filtrate passes through the filter paper and is collected into the China dish placed below. The insoluble impurities are left behind on the filter paper.

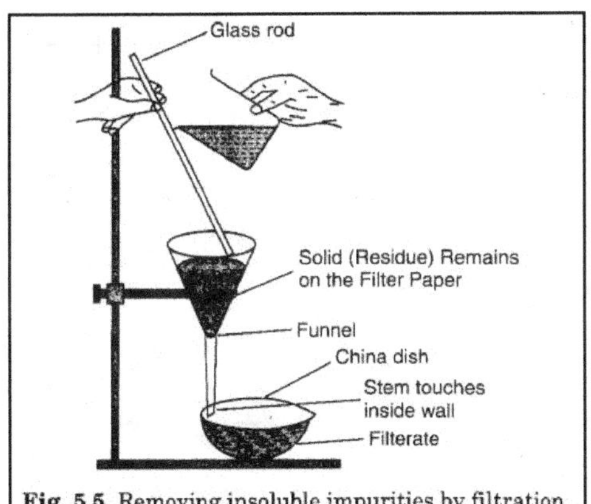

Fig. 5.5. Removing insoluble impurities by filtration.

3. CONCENTRATION OF FILTRATE

a. Place the dish containing the clear filtrate over wire gauze, kept over a tripod stand and heat it gently (Do not boil). Stir the solution with a glass rod (Fig. 5.6). This is done to ensure uniform evaporation and to prevent formation of solid crust.

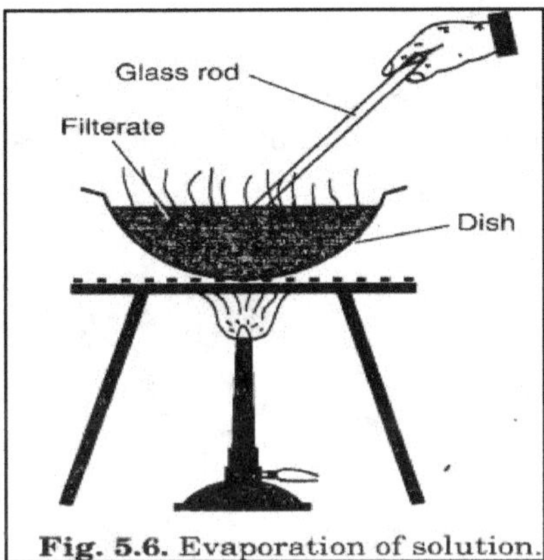

Fig. 5.6. Evaporation of solution.

b. When the volume of the solution is reduced to one-half, take out a drop of the concentrated solution on one end of glass rod and cool it by blowing air (Fig. 5.7). Formation of thin crust indicates that **crystallisation point** has reached.

c. Stop heating by removing the Burner.

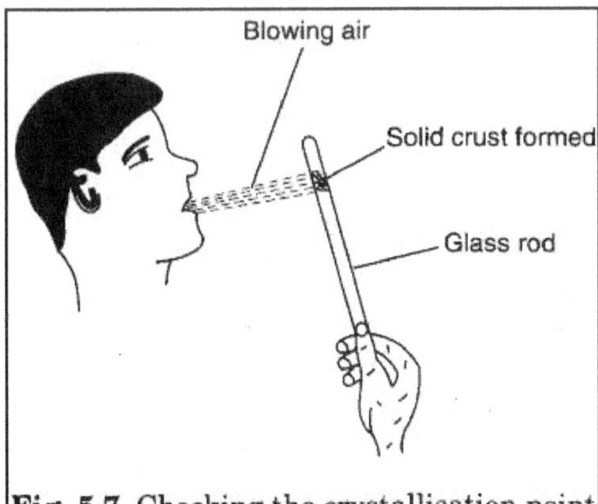

Fig. 5.7. Checking the crystallisation point

4. COOLING THE CONCENTRATED SOLUTION

a. Pour the concentrated solution into a crystallizing dish. (It is a thin walled shallow glass dish with a flat bottom and vertical sides. It has a spout to pour off the mother liquor).

b. Cover the dish with a watch glass and keep it undisturbed.

c. As the solution cools, crystals separate out. The concentrated solution is cooled slowly for better yield of the crystals.

Sometimes the China dish containing the concentrated solution is cooled by placing on a beaker filled to the brim with cold water Fig. 5.8. Cooling may also be done by keeping the China dish in open air depending upon the weather conditions.

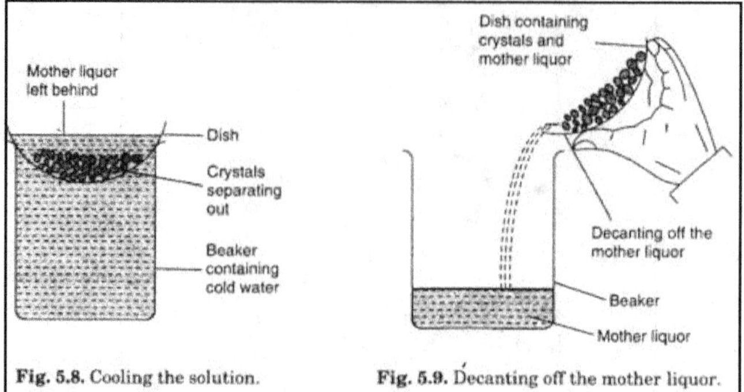

Fig. 5.8. Cooling the solution.   **Fig. 5.9.** Decanting off the mother liquor.

5. SEPARATION AND DRYING OF CRYSTALS

a. Decant off the mother liquor Fig. 5.9, and wash the crystals with cold water or alcohol.

b. Dry the crystals by pressing them gently between the sheets of filter paper Fig. 5.10. The crystals can be dried by spreading them on a porous plate for some time or by placing the crystals in vacuum desiccator. Crystals have definite geometry and a definite shape. Fig. 5.11 shows some of these shapes. Copper sulphate crystals are formed in triclinic shape, potash alum comes out in octahedral geometry. Potassium nitrate crystals are needle like and ferrous sulphate have monoclinic shape.

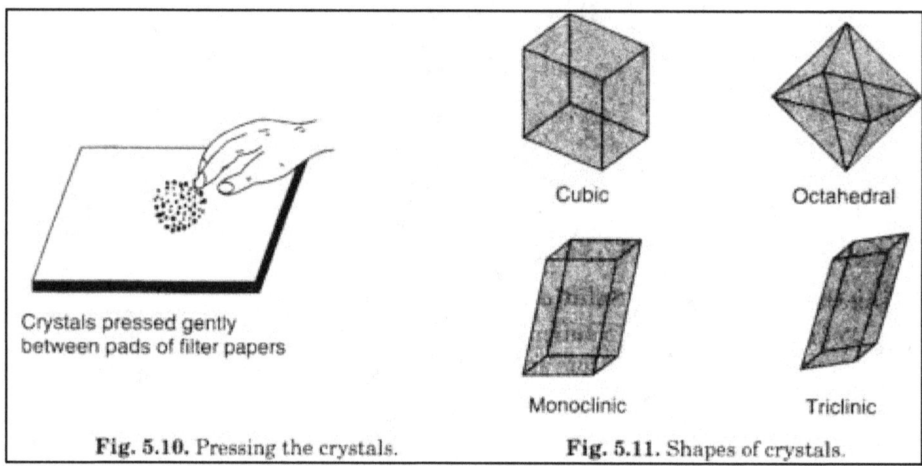

Fig. 5.10. Pressing the crystals.   **Fig. 5.11.** Shapes of crystals.

Experiment 3

AIM

To prepare crystals of pure potash from the commercial sample.

MATERIAL REQUIRED

250ml beaker, China dish, measuring cylinder, glass rod, funnel, Burner, tripod stand, wire gauze.

PROCEDURE

Potash alum (Fitrakis) is highly soluble in water. The commercial sample is shaken with water when alum dissolves. The insoluble impurities are removed by filtration. The solution is concentrated and then cooled. On cooling pure crystals of alum separate. The soluble impurities are left behind in the mother liquor.

1. PREPARATION OF SOLUTION

Take a 400 ml beaker. Put in it about 5-6 gm of the crude sample of potash alum and 25-30 ml water. Stir the contents of the beaker to make the solution clear. Warm to dissolve the whole of alum present in the sample.

2. FILTRATION OF THE SOLUTION AND CONCENTRATION OF THE FILTRATE TO CRYSTALLISATION POINT

Filter the solution and collect the filtrate in a China dish. The insoluble impurities are left as residue on the filter paper.

Heat the China dish on a sand bath/wire gauge till the solution is reduced to about one- third of its original volume. As the solution gets heated up, it is stirred well with a glass rod to avoid crust formation on the side of the dish. If the crust is formed, it is dissolved into the solution by removing it with glass rod.

Take out a drop of the solution at the end of glass rod and cool it by blowing. The appearance of a thin crust on the glass rod shows that the crystallization point has reached. Stop heating at this stage by removing the Burner. Transfer the hot saturated solution in a crystallizing dish.

3. COOLING THE HOT SATURATED SOLUTION

Place the dish containing hot saturated solution on a beaker containing water filled to the brim and allow it to cool slowly for some time. Colorless, transparent and octahedral crystals of alum begin to separate. After about half an hour, the crystallization is complete.

4. SEPARATION OF CRYSTALS AND DRYING

Decant off the mother liquor carefully. Wash the crystals with cold solution of alcohol and water. Remove the crystals on a filter paper which soaks the solution. Transfer the crystals on another filter paper and dry them by pressing gently between the folds of the filter papers. Transfer the crystals to a dry test tube and cork it.

RESULT

The crystals of pure potash alum are colorless, transparent and octahedral.

PREACAUTION

1. The filtrate should be evaporated slowly by gently heating during concentration.
2. The filtrate is to be evaporated only up to the crystallization point. It should never be heated to dryness. Avoid over heating of the solution.
3. The solution should be cooled slowly without disturbing it. It should never be cooled rapidly.
4. Wash the crystals with the washing liquid 3-4 times using very small amount of the liquid each time.
5. In case the crystals obtained are very small, it means that the solution has been concentrated more than that required at the crystallization stage.

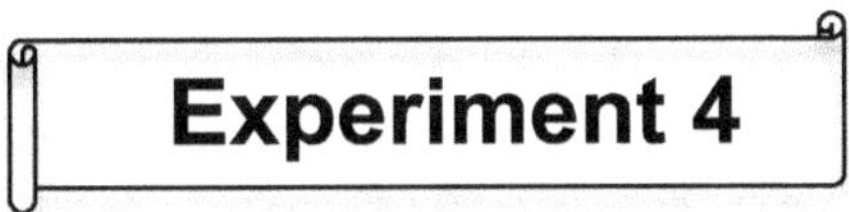

AIM

To prepare crystals of copper sulphate from commercial sample of copper sulphate (blue vitriol)

MATERIAL REQUIREMENT

Powdered copper sulphate (crude sample), distilled water, dil. H_2SO_4 and filter paper, funnel

PROCEDURE

The given sample is shaken with water. A few drops of dilute sulfuric acid are added to it in order to prevent hydrolysis of copper sulphate. Copper sulphate present in the sample gets dissolved while the insoluble impurities are left behind. The solution is filtered. The filtrate is concentrated to the crystallisation point and then cooled. On cooling, crystals of copper sulphate ($CuSO_4.5H_2O$) separate out.

1. PREPARATION OF SOLUTION

Take about 25-30 ml of water and add to it small quantities of the powdered crude copper sulphate. Stir well to dissolve it. Make several additions of the powdered sample till a little of it remains undissolved even if it is stirred for some time. Now add 2-3 ml of dilute sulfuric acid to make the solution clear. This prevents hydrolysis of the copper sulphate.

2. FILTRATION OF THE SOLUTION AND CONCENTRATION OF THE FILTRATE TO CRYSTALLISATION POINT

Filter the solution and collect the filtrate in China impurities are left as residue on the filter paper.

Heat the China dish on a sand bath till the solution is reduced to about one-third of its original volume. As the solution gets heated up, it is stirred well with a glass rod to avoid crust formation on the side of the dish. If the crust is formed, it is dissolved into the solution by removing it with glass rod. Don't allow the solution in the dish to boil.

Remove a drop of the solution at the end of a glass rod and cool it by blowing. The appearance of a crust or tiny crystals on the glass rod shows that the crystallisation point has reached. Now turn off the Burner and stop heating. Transfer the hot saturated solution in a crystallizing dish.

3. COOLING THE HOT SATURATED SOLUTION

Place the crystallization dish containing hot saturated solution on a beaker containing water filled to the brim and allow it to cool slowly for some time. Deep blue crystals of copper sulphate will appear. After about half an hour, the crystallisation is complete.

Fig. 5.12. Preserving of crystals.

SEPARATION OF CRYSTALS AND DRYING

Decant off the mother liquor carefully. Wash the crystals with a little ethyl alcohol containing small amount of cold water. Remove the crystals on a filter paper which soaks the solution. Transfer the crystals on another filter paper and dry them by pressing gently between the folds of the filter papers or by spreading on a porous plate. Transfer the crystals to a dry test tube and cork it (Fig. 5.12).

RESULT

The crystals of pure copper sulphate ($CuSO_4.5H_2O$) are triclinic, transparent and blue

PRECAUTION

1. The filtrate should be evaporated slowly by gently heating during concentration.
2. The filtrate is to be evaporated only up to the crystallization point. It should never be heated to dryness. Avoid over heating of the solution.
3. The solution should be cooled slowly without disturbing it. It should never be cooled rapidly.
4. Wash the crystals with the washing liquid 3-4 times using very small amount of the liquid each time.
5. In case the crystals obtained are very small, it means that the solution has been concentrated more than that required at the crystallisation stage.

Experiment 5

Aim
To prepare benzoic acid crystals from the crude sample.

MATERIAL REQUIRED
China dish, funnel, Burner, tripod stand beaker.

PROCEDURE
Benzoic acid is a crystalline solid that has moderate solubility in hot water and low solubility in cold water. Its structure is:

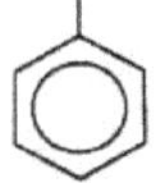

Benzoic acid is recrystallised by dissolving it in hot water.

PROCEDURE

1. **PREPARATION OF SOLUTION**

   Take about 150 ml of water in a 250 ml beaker and keep it for boiling using tripod stand and wire gauze. In another 250 ml beaker take 2-3 gm of the crude sample of benzoic acid and add gradually with stirring minimum quantity of boiling water just sufficient to dissolve benzoic acid. Heating can be done if required.

2. **FILTRATION OF THE SOLUTION**

   Filter the hot solution immediately using fluted filter paper placed in a funnel. Insoluble impurities are left on the filter paper.

3. **COOLING THE HOT SATURATED SOLUTION**

   Let the filtered solution come to room temperature by itself. Now cool it by placing in cold water trough.

4. **SEPARATION OF CRYSTALS AND DRYING**

   Separate the crystals by Alteration using funnel and filter paper. Wash the crystals with cold water. Transfer the crystals on another filter paper and dry them by pressing gently between the folds of a filter paper. Transfer the crystals to a dry test tube and cork it.

RESULT
The crystals of benzoic acid are opaque white.
Color - colorless
Yield of the crystals = g

PRECAUTION
1. The vapor of benzene should be away from flame.
2. Heating should be done only on water bath.

Question.1. Define melting point.
Answer. It is defined as the constant temperature at which the solid and the liquid phases of substance coexist.

Question.2. How is the determination of melting point useful?
Answer. It helps us to:
(i) identify unknown substances;
(ii) know whether a compound is pure or not.

Question.3. How does the determination of melting point help us know about the purity of the compound?
Answer. Melting point indicates the purity of a substance. If a substance contains moisture or some other impurity, then its melting point is usually lowered. A sharp melting point indicates a pure substance.

Question.4. What is sharp melting point?
Answer. Melting point of a solid is said to be sharp if it melts completely within a range of 1°C.

Question.5. Why do pure solids possess sharp melting point?
Answer. A pure solid has same force of attraction between particles at different places and hence melts at a constant temperature.

Question.6. What is the effect of impurities on the melting point of solids?
Answer. Impurities lower the melting point of a solid.

Question.7. Can we heat the capillary tube directly for the determination of melting point?
Answer. No, because direct heating would result in uneven and fast heating.

Question.8. Can any other liquid be used in place of liquid paraffin to determine the melting point?
Answer. Yes, concentrated H_2SO_4 or silicone oils can be used to determine the melting point.

Question.9. Why is the melting point of benzamide more than that of acetamide?
Answer. Benzamide and acetamide contain same functional group, but the molecular mass of benzamide is more than that of acetamide. As a result, benzamide has stronger intermolecular forces and hence has higher melting point.

Question.10. Why different solids have different melting points?
Answer. Melting point depends upon intermolecular forces existing in the solid state. Since different solids have intermolecular forces of different strength, their melting points are different.

Question.11. Define boiling point.
Answer. Boiling point may be defined as the temperature at which the vapor pressure of the liquid becomes equal to the atmospheric pressure.

Question.12. What is the effect of increase of pressure on the boiling point?
Answer. On increasing the outside pressure, the boiling point of liquid increases.

Question.13. What is the effect of decrease of pressure on the boiling point?
Answer. On decreasing the outside pressure, the boiling point of liquid decreases.

Question.14. What will happen to the boiling point of the liquid if some non-volatile liquid is added to it?
Answer. The boiling point of the liquid will increase.

Question.15. Why different liquids have different boiling points?
Answer. Boiling point depends upon intermolecular forces existing in the liquid. Since different liquids have intermolecular forces of different strength therefore their boiling points are different.

Question.16. Why is food cooked more quickly in a pressure cooker?
Answer. In a pressure cooker water boils at a higher temperature and hence cooking takes place at a higher temperature.

Question.17. Suppose boiling point of a liquid is 100°C in Delhi. At hill station will it be the same or different? Give reasons.

Answer. The boiling point of the liquid will be less than 100°C at the hill station. Boiling point decreases with decrease in atmospheric pressure. At hill stations the atmospheric pressure is less than that in plains.

Question.18. What is the difference between a glass tube and glass rod?
Answer. A glass tube is hollow from inside while a glass rod is solid.

Question.19. Why should cork be wetted before pressing?
Answer. Cork is wetted to avoid its cracking and to make it soft.

Question.20. Why is Bunsen Burner provided with air holes?
Answer. To regulate the supply of air to the gas.

Question.21. What type of flame is generally used for heating purposes?
Answer. Oxidizing blue flame is used since it gives maximum heat due to complete combustion of fuel.

Question.22. What is the use of a glass tube jet?
Answer. A glass tube jet can be used to make droppers.

Question.23. Where does bent glass tube needed?
Answer. Bent glass tubes are required during preparation and collection of gases, for passing the gas through solutions, for making salt bridges, etc.

Question.24. What is the use of a triangular file?
Answer. Triangular file is used to make serrate on the glass rod or tube during its cutting.

Question.25. What type of material is glass; amorphous or crystalline?
Answer. Glass is an amorphous substance.

Question.26. Define the term 'crystallisation'.
Answer. The substances when present in well-defined geometrical shapes are called crystals. These are formed when a hot saturated solution of the salt is allowed to cool slowly and undisturbed. This process is termed as crystallisation.

Question.27. What is solubility?
Answer. It is the amount of the solute which when dissolved in 100 gm of the solvent provides a saturated solution.

Question.28. Why is crystallisation done?
Answer. Crystallisation enables to prepare a substance in state of highest purity.

Question.29. What is filtration?
Answer. It is a process of separating insoluble substances by passing the solution through a filter paper.

Question.30. What is Kipp's waste?
Answer. It is a' mixture left behind after production of H_2S gas by reaction between $FeSO_4$ and dilute H_2SO_4. It mainly contains $FeSO_4$ and unreacted dilute H_2SO_4.

Question.31. What is meant by the term, 'water of crystallisation'?
Answer. Water of crystallisation is the definite number of water molecules that is present in lose combination with one formula unit of the compound.

Question.32. Explain the term—saturated solution.
Answer. A solution in which no more of solute can be dissolved at a particular temperature is known as saturated solution.

Question.33. Why is solution not heated to dryness to get crystals?
Answer. Heating the solution to dryness will not remove soluble impurities and crystals of very poor quality are obtained.

Question.34. What is characteristic of crystals?
Answer. Crystals have well defined geometry and shape.

Question.35. Why is the hot saturated solution not cooled suddenly?
Answer. By allowing saturated solution to cool slowly, crystals grow in size. It helps in their better separation as units rather than giving a massy substance of no proper geometry.

Question.36. What is the term 'seeding'?
Answer. Sometimes on cooling the saturated solution, crystallisation does not occur. A crystal of same substance is placed in the saturated solution which causes seeding. It helps in quick separation of crystals from saturated solution.

Question.37. What is green vitriol?
Answer. It is hydrated ferrous sulphate $FeSO_4.7H_2O$.

Question.38. What is mother liquor?
Answer. The liquid left behind after the separation of crystals from a saturated solution is known as mother liquor.

Question.39. Name the different steps involved in the process of crystallisation?
Answer. The various steps are:
(i) Preparation of the solution.
(ii) Filtration of the solution.
(iii) Concentration of the solution.
(iv) Cooling of the solution slowly.
(v) Separation and drying of the crystals.

Question.40. What are the formulae of blue vitriol, potash alum and green vitriol crystals?
Answer. The formulae are ($CuSO_4.5H_2O$), ($K_2SO_4.Al_2(SO_4)_3.24H_2O$), $FeSO_4.7H_2O$.

Question.41. What is the formula of benzoic acid?
Answer.

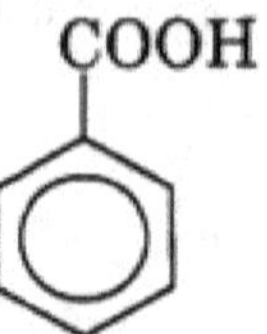

Question.43. What is the effect of temperature on ionic product of water?
Answer. The values of $[H_3O^+]$ and $[OH^-]$ are always equal at all temperatures but the value of K_w is different at different temperature. K_w increases on increase in temperature.

Question.44. What is value of K_w at 298K?
Answer. The value of K_w at 298K is 1×10^{-14}.

Question.45. What is the pH of pure water at?
Answer. pH of pure water is 7.

Question.46. What is an acid base indicator?
Answer. An acid base indicator is an organic compound which changes its color within a range of pH. It is used in titrations to indicate the excess of acid or base in the solution.

Question.47. What is a pH paper?
Answer. pH paper is a strip of paper which is prepared by dipping the strip in the solutions of different indicators and then drying them.

Question.48. What do you predict about the pH of orange juice?
Answer. Since orange juice contains vitamin C i.e ascorbic acid. Hence the pH should be less than 7.

Question.49. Name the commonly used indicator in acid-base titrations.
Answer. Phenolphthalein and methyl orange.

Question.50. What is a strong and a weak acid?
Answer. An acid which dissociates into ions

completely is called a strong acid but a weak acid does not completely dissociate in aqueous solutions

Question.42. What happens when the following crystals are heated separately?
(i) Blue vitriol
(ii) Potash alum
(iii) Benzoic acid
Answer. (i) It changes into white powder due to loss of water of crystallisation.
(ii) It changes into fluffy white mass.
(iii) It undergoes sublimation.

e.g., hydrochloric acid is a strong acid and acetic acid is a weak acid.

Question.51. Why is pH of $0.1MHCl$ and $0.1MCH_3COOH$ different?
Answer. Because HCl is a strong acid and CH_3COOH is a weak acid. 0.1M of each will furnish different amount of $[H^+]$ ions and hence will have different pH.

Question.52. What is universal indicator solution?
Answer. It is prepared by mixing a number of common indicators together so that mixture obtained can undergo a series of changes over a much wider pH range.

Question.53. What is common ion effect?
Answer. Common ion effect is the suppression of degree of dissociation of weak electrolyte in presence of strong electrolyte having a common ion in it.

EXPERIMENTS BASED ON pH CHANGE

pH SCALE

In order to express the hydronium ion (H_3O^+) concentration in a solution P.L. Sorensen (1909) devised a logarithmic scale. This scale is known as pH scale. The pH of a solution is defined as the negative logarithm of hydronium ion concentration in moles per liter.

$pH = -\log[H_3O^+]$

$= \log_1 H_3O^+$

Acidity, Alkalinity, Neutrality of Solutions

NEUTRAL SOLUTION

$H^+ = OH^- = 10^{-7}M; pH = -7$

ACIDIC SOLUTION

$H^+ > OH^-$, $H^+ > 10^{-7}M$, $pH < 7$.

BASIC SOLUTION

$OH^- > H^+$, $H^+ < 10^{-7}M$, $pH > 7$. (Also called an alkaline solution)

STRONG AND WEAK ACIDS AND BASES

STRONG ACID

An acid that is a strong electrolyte and has a pH < 3.
For example: H_2SO_4, HCl, HBr, HI, HNO_3

WEAK ACID

An acid that is a weak electrolyte or an ionic compound that partially reacts with water to form hydrogen ions in aqueous solution. It will have a pH greater than 3 but less than 7.
For example, H_2S, H_3PO_4, CH_3COOH, H_2CO_3.

STRONG BASE

A hydroxide that is a strong electrolyte and has a pH >11.
For example: NaOH, KOH, Ba $(OH)_2$.

WEAK BASE

A hydroxide that is a weak electrolyte or a compound that partially reacts with water to form hydroxide ions in aqueous solution. Its pH will be less than 11 but greater than 7.
For example: carbonates, bicarbonates, ammonia (ammonium hydroxide), phosphates.

SALT

An ionic compound produced by reacting an acid and a base. It will have a pH close to 7.

IONIC PRODUCT OF WATER

Pure water is very weakly ionised. So, there is an equilibrium between ionised and unionised molecules.

$2H_2O(l) \rightleftharpoons H_3O^+(aq) + OH^-(aq)$

The equilibrium constant, $K = \dfrac{[H_3O^+][OH^-]}{[H_2O]^2}$

As concentration of water is very large so it practically remains constant.

$$\text{Thus,} \quad K[H_2O]^2 = [H_3O^+][OH^-]$$
$$K_w = [H_3O^+][OH^-]$$

where, K_w is the ionic product of water. The value of K_w at 298K is $1.0 \times 10^{-14} mol^2 L^{-2}$.

$$\therefore \quad 1.0 \times 10^{-14} = [H_3O^+][OH^-]$$

As one mole of water gives one mole of H_3O^+ and one mole of OH^- ions.

$$\therefore \quad [H_3O^+] = [OH^-]$$
$$\text{Thus,} \quad 1.0 \times 10^{-14} = [H_3O^+]^2$$
$$\text{or} \quad [H_3O^+] = 1.0 \times 10^{-7} molL^{-1}$$
$$\text{Now} \quad pH = -\log [H_3O^+]$$
$$= -\log (1.0 \times 10^{-7}) = 7$$

In general, it has been observed that at room temperature all neutral solutions have pH equal to 7, all acidic solutions have pH less than 7 and all basic solutions have pH more than 7.

COMMON ION EFFECT

Common ion effect may be defined as the suppression of degree of dissociation of a weak electrolyte by the addition of a small amount of some strong electrolyte having a common ion with that of the weak electrolyte. Consider for example, NH_4OH which is a weak electrolyte and there is an equilibrium between unionised molecules and its ions.

$$NH_4OH \rightleftharpoons NH_4^+ + OH^-$$

When NH_4Cl, a strong electrolyte, is added to it, NH_4Cl ionises as

$$NH_4Cl \longrightarrow NH_4^+ + Cl^-$$

Due to the presence of common NH_4^+ ions the equilibrium (6.1) shifts in the backward direction and degree of dissociation of NH_4OH is suppressed. So, the concentration of OH^- ions decreases and hence concentration of H_3O^+ ions increase. Thus, pH of the solution is lowered.

Similarly consider acetic acid, a weak electrolyte

$$CH_3COOH \rightleftharpoons CH_3O^- + H^+CO$$

When sodium acetate, a strong electrolyte is added to it CH_3COONa ionises as:

$$CH_3COONa \longrightarrow CH_3COO^- + Na^+$$

Due to the presence of common CH_3COO^- ions the equilibrium (6.2) shifts in the backward direction and so concentration of H_3O^+ ions decreases and hence that of OH^- ions increases. Therefore, pH of solution increases.

Salts when dissolved in water may undergo hydrolysis producing acidic or basic solutions. Hydrolysis of salts may be defined as the interaction of ions of the salt with water producing acidic or basic solution.

Hydrolysis of salts of strong bases and weak acids produces alkaline solution on hydrolysis. For example, the aqueous solution of sodium acetate is alkaline due to the presence of excess hydroxyl ions in the solution.

$$\underset{\text{Sodium acetate}}{CH_3COONa} + H_2O \rightleftharpoons \underset{\substack{\text{Acetic acid} \\ \text{(weakly ionised)}}}{CH_3COOH} + Na^+ + OH^-$$

Hydrolysis of salts of strong acids and weak bases produces acidic solution due to the presence of excess hydronium ions in the solution. For example, an aqueous solution of ammonium chloride is acidic in nature.

$$\underset{\text{Ammonium chloride}}{NH_4Cl} + 2H_2O \rightleftharpoons \underset{\text{(weakly ionised)}}{NH_4OH} + H_3O^+ + Cl^-$$

Hydrolysis of salts of weak acids and weak bases gives almost neutral solutions. For example,

$$CH_3COONH_4 + H_2O \rightleftharpoons CH_3COOH + NH_4OH$$

Ammonium acetate

Salts of strong acids and strong bases do not undergo hydrolysis and hence their aqueous solutions are neutral.

Table 6.1. Color Changes and pH range of Certain Indicators

S. No..	Indicator	pH range	Color in acidic medium	Color in alkaline medium
1.	Thymol blue	1.2-2.8	Red	Yellow
2.	Methyl yellow	2.9-4.0	Red	Yellow
3.	Bromophenol blue	3.0-4.6	Yellow	Blue
4.	Congo red	3.0-5.0	Violet	Red
5.	Methyl orange	3.1-4.4	Red	Yellow
6.	Methyl red	4.2-6.3	Red	Yellow
7.	Phenol red	6.8-8.4	Yellow	Red
8.	Phenolphthalein	8.3-10.0	Colorless	Pink
9.	Thymolphthalein	9.4-10.5	Colorless	Blue

UNIVERSAL INDICATOR

A universal indicator is prepared by mixing a number of common indicators together so that the mixture obtained can pass through a series of color changes over a much wider pH range. For example, one such mixture which may show various colors at different pH is as given in Table 6.2.

Table 6.2. Colors of Universal Indicator at Different pH Values

pH	Color
3.0	Red
5.0	Orange red
5.5	Orange
6.0	Orange-yellow
7.0-7.5	Greenish-yellow
8.0	Green
9.5	Blue
10.0	Violet

Such mixtures are commonly known as universal indicators. Universal indicators are available commercially as solutions and as test papers. A pH paper is a strip of paper which is prepared by dipping the strip in the solutions of different indicators and then drying them.

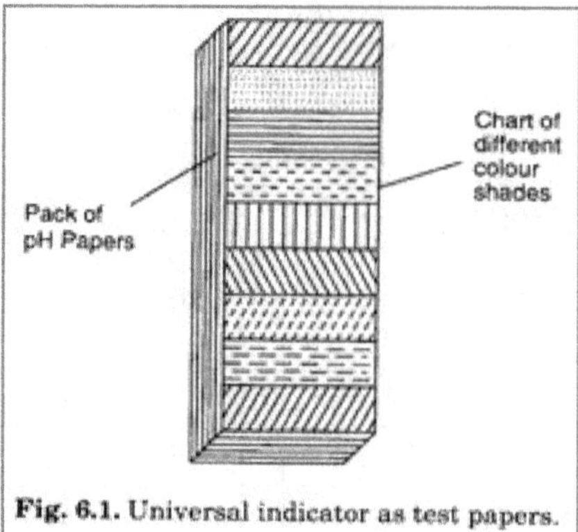

Fig. 6.1. Universal indicator as test papers.

pH paper can be used to find the approximate pH of any solution. The pH paper is dipped in a given sample of the solution, the color developed in the paper is compared with the color chart and approximate pH of the solution can be predicted. A pH paper is shown in Fig. 6.1.

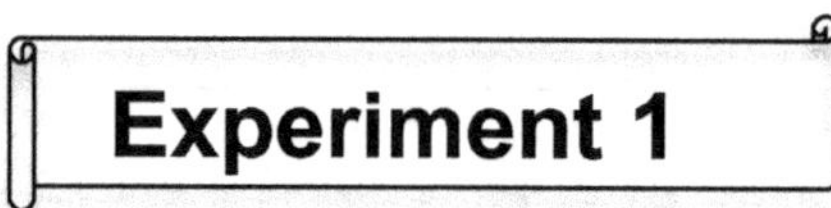

Experiment 1

AIM

To determine the pH of vegetables and fruit juices and acids and bases of known and varied concentration using pH paper.

MATERIAL REQUIREMENT

Test tube, dropper, measuring cylinder.

PROCEDURE

1. Using pH Paper. Take some clean and dry test tubes and place various samples of vegetable and fruit juices in each of them.
   Now put one or two drops of each sample on different strips of pH papers Note the color formed on each strip and compare the shade with those on color chart. Record the pH of the compared shade.
2. Using Indicator Solution. Take 10 ml of different juices in different test tubes with the help of measuring cylinder. Put a few drops of universal indicator in each of them. Note the color of each solution and compare with those on indicator bottle. Record the approximate pH of each.

OBSERVATION

pH of Vegetable and Fruit juices

Sample	For pH paper		For indicator solution	
	Color produced on pH paper	Approximate pH	Color produced in solution	Approximate pH
Lemon juice				
Tomato juice				
Orange juice				
Pineapple juice				

| Amla juice | | | | |
| Mango juice | | | | |

RESULT

pH of --------, -------, --------, -------- etc. are less than seven and are acidic sample.

pH of-------, ------- etc. are more than 7 and hence are basic samples.

PRECAUTION

1. Equal no of drops of universal indicator should be added in each test tube.
2. Color change should be matched carefully.

AIM

To compare the pH of solution of strong and weak acid of same concentration.

MATERIAL REQUIRED

Test tube, pipette, test tube stand, dropper, 0.1 M HCL and 0.1 M acetic acid

PROCEDURE

A strong acid is completely ionised in aqueous solution. It produces higher concentration of hydrogen ions for a given concentration of the acid as compared with a weak acid and hence has lower pH.

1. Take four clean and dry test tubes and half fill each of the tubes with one of the acid solutions.
2. Take 5ml of 0.1 M HCl and 5ml of 0.1 M CH_3COOH in separate test tube.
3. Put a drop of 0.1 M HCl on pH paper and note the color as in experiment 1. Repeat with 0.1 M CH_3COOH solution also.

OBSERVATION

Sample	Concentration	Color	pH
HCl	0.1M	-	-
CH_3COOH	0.1M	-	-

RESULT

pH of 0.1 M HCL solution (strong acid) is_________.

pH of 0.1 CH_3COOH (Weak acid) is_________.

PRECAUTION

1. Add equal number of drops of the universal indicator to equal amounts of solution in each of the boiling tubes.
2. Match the color of the solution with pH chart carefully.

AIM

To study the pHchange in the titration of a strong base with a strong acid using universal indicator.

MATERIAL REQUIRED

burette, pipette(10ml), Conical flask, dropper, white tile, funnel, universal indicator, 0.1 M NaOH, 0.1 M HCl, 1 M NaOH, 1 M HCl, 0.5 M NaOH, 0.5 M HCl

PROCEDURE

1. Fill up the burette with 1 M NaOH solution. Note down the initial burette reading.
2. Pipette out 10ml of 1 M HCl solution. Note down the initial burette reading.
3. Add few drops of universal indicator.
4. Note down the color of the solution in the conical flask and note down the pH.
5. Run down NaOH from the burette slowly and note the change in the color of the solution.
6. Record the volume of NaOH used for every color change.
7. Record your observations.
8. At the end point when the amount of HCl has been completely neutralized by NaOH, the extra drop of strong alkali will give purple coloration due to high pH. Range 12-14.

OBSERVATION

Solution in conical flask = 10 ml of 1 M HCl.

OBSERVATION TABLE

S. NO..	VOLUME OF NaOH	COLOR OF THE SOLUTION	pH range

RESULT

There is a gradual change in the color in the beginning as the pH is varying gradually due to the addition of NaOH dropwise. This NaOH is being used by HCl gradually. At the end point there is sudden change in color to purple (the solution will be alkaline). The final color will be different in end points using (0.1 M NaOH, 0.1 M HCl) and (0.5 M NaOH, 0.5 M HCl).

PRECAUTION

1. Use small amount and equal number of drops of indicators every time.
2. Keep the conical flask over a white paper so that the change in color is easily available.

AIM

(a) **To study the change in pH of acetic acid (a weak acid) solution by addition of sodium acetate.**
(b) **To study the change in pH of ammonium hydroxide (a weak base) solution by the addition of ammonium chloride.**

MATERIAL REQUIRED

Test tubes, test tube stand, watch glass, pH paper, glass rod, for experiment:
a. acetic acid and sodium acetate and for experiment
b. ammonium hydroxide and ammonium chloride.

PROCEDURE

a) Acetic acid is a weak acid and is only slightly ionised. On the addition of sodium acetate which is strong electrolyte the concentration of acetate ions increases.

$$CH_3COOH + H_2O \rightleftharpoons CH_3COO^- + H_3O^+$$

$$CH_3COONa \longrightarrow CH_3COO^- + Na^+$$

The increase in concentration of acetate ions shifts the equilibrium (6.3) in backward direction. Due to this, the concentration of H_3O^+ ions decreases and hence pH of solution increases.

b) Ammonium hydroxide is a weak base and is partially dissociated. When ammonium chloride, a strong electrolyte is added to it, the concentration of NH_4^+ ions increase.

$$NH_4OH \rightleftharpoons NH_4^+ + OH^-$$

$$NH_4Cl \longrightarrow NH_4^+ + Cl^-$$

Due to increase in concentration of NH_4^+ ions the equilibrium (6.5) shifts in the backward direction and concentration of OH^- ions fall. This means concentration of H_3O^+ ions increases and hence pH decreases.

1. In a dry and clean test tube take 10 ml of acetic acid solution. Put a drop of this solution on a strip of pH paper and note its color. Compare it with the color on chart paper and note pH of the acid.
2. Now weigh 1 g of sodium acetate and put it in the tube containing acetic acid. Shake vigorously to dissolve sodium acetate. Determine pH of this solution with pH paper.
3. Weigh again 1 g of sodium acetate, add to test tube and determine pH of this solution.
4. Repeat this with more of sodium acetate and find out the change in pH value.

OBSERVATION

S. No..	Sample solution	Color produced on pH paper	Approximate pH value
1.	CH_3COOH		
2.	$CH_3COOH + 1\ g\ CH_3COONa$		
3.	$CH_3COOH + 2\ g\ CH_3COONa$		
4.	$CH_3COOH + 3\ g\ CH_3COONa$		

RESULT

The pH value of solution goes on increasing on adding more and more of sodium acetate.

1. Take 10 ml of **ammonium hydroxide solution** in a test tube. Put a drop of this on pH paper and note the color. Compare the color produced with the color on chart paper and note its pH value.
2. Now weigh 1.5 g of NH_4Cl and put in the tube containing NH_4OH. Shake vigorously and note the pH with the help of pH paper.
3. Repeat the experiment by adding two more samples of 1.5 g each of NH_4Cl.

Note:
If there is any change in pH value.

S. No..	Sample solution	Color produced on pH paper	Approximate pH value
1.	NH_4OH		
2.	$NH_4OH + 1.5$ g NH_4Cl		
3.	$NH_4OH + 3.0$ g NH_4Cl		
4.	$NH_4OH + 4.5$ g NH_4Cl		

RESULT

The pH of NH_4OH decreases with addition of NH_4Cl to it.

PRECAUTION

1. Equal number of drops should be put on the pH solution.
2. The compound added should be completely dissolved before noting the pH.

Question.1. Define pH.
Answer. It is defined as the negative logarithm of hydronium ion concentration in moles per liter. $pH = -\log [H_3O^+]$

Question.2. What do you mean by pOH?
Answer. It is negative logarithm of OH^- ion concentration.
$pOH = -\log [OH^-] = 14 - pH.$

Question.3. What is pH of pure water at 25°C?
Answer. 7

Question.4. What does pH of a solution signify?
Answer. It signifies the H_3O^+ ion concentration in moles per liter.

Question.5. What is pH of a solution if it is acidic?
Answer. pH of an acidic solution is less than 7.

Question.6. Write self ionisation of water. What is the value of ionic product of water at 298 K?
Answer. $H_2O + H_2O \rightleftharpoons H_3O^+ + OH^-$
The value of ionic product of water at 298 K $= 1.0 \times 10^{-14} \, mol^2 \, L^{-2}$

Question.7. What is ionic product of water?
Answer. $K_w = [H_3O^+] [OH^-].$

Question.8. Is pH of pure water affected by rise in temperature?
Answer. The pH value slightly decreases with the rise in temperature. This is due to increase in degree of dissociation of water with rise in temperature which in turn results in increase in the concentration of hydronium ions.

Question.9. Is the value of ionic product of water affected by addition of acid or base?
Answer. No, if a little of acid is added its H_3O^+ ion concentration increases and correspondingly OH^- ion concentration decreases. Thus, ionic product of water remains same.

Question.10. What happens to the pH of the solution if a little acid is added to water?
Answer. When a little acid is added then concentration of H_3O^+ ions in the solution increases. Thus, pH of the solution decreases.

Question.11. 10 ml. lemon juice is diluted with an equal volume of water. What effect is likely to be observed on the pH of the solution?
Answer. The pH of the solution (diluted lemon juice) would be more than that of pure lemon juice.

Question.12. Out of lemon juice and apple juice which one would have lower pH?
Answer. Lemon juice would have lower pH as it is more acidic.

Question.13. If any two acidic solutions are mixed what would happen to the pH of the mixture?
Answer. pH of the mixture would lie in between the pH values of the two solutions.

Question.14. What is the effect of dilution on pH of (i) an acidic solution (ii) a basic solution.
Answer? (i) pH of an acidic solution increases on dilution (ii) pH of a basic solution decrease on dilution.

Question.15. Will the pH of 0.1 M acetic acid be the same as that of 0.1 M hydrochloric acid?
Answer. pH of 0.1 M acetic acid would be more than pH of 0.1 M HCl because acetic acid, being a weak acid, is only partially ionised and hence produces lower cone, of H_3O^+ (aq).

Question.16. What is an acid-base indicator?
Answer. An acid-base indicator is an organic compound which changes its color within certain pH range.

Question.17. What do you mean by universal indicator?
Answer. It is a mixture of several indicators having different pH ranges. It shows many color changes over a wide range of pH. Each color corresponds to a certain approximate pH.

Question.18. What is the relationship between pH and pOH of an aqueous solution?
Answer. The relationship is
$pH + pOH = pK_w = 14$ (at 298 K)

Question.19. Does addition of a salt having a common ion to a weak acid change the pH of the solution?
Answer. Yes, the pH of the solution increases.

Question.20. The pH of a solution is 4.5. How does this solution affect a litmus paper?
Answer. The solution is acidic and it will turn blue litmus red.

Question.21. What do you think about pH of lemon juice or orange juice?
Answer. The lemon juice or orange juice contains vitamin C which is ascorbic acid. The solution being acidic has pH less than 7.

Question.22. Calculate the pH of NaOH solution which is 1 x 10^{-14} M.

Answer. Assuming that NaOH is fully ionised

$[OH^-] = 1 \times 10^{-14}$ mol^2 L^{-1}

Now $K_w = [H_3O^+] [OH^-]$

or $\quad 10^{-14} = [H_3O^+] [10^{-4}]$

or $\quad [H_3O^+] = 10{-14}10{-4} = 10^{-10}$ mol L^{-1}

$pH = - \log [H_3O^+]$

$= - \log [10^{-10}] = 10$

Question.23. Which of the following solutions has lower pH: 0.1 M HCl or 0.1 M CH$_3$COOH?

Answer. 0.1 M HCl would have lower pH because HCl being a strong acid produces higher concentration of hydronium ions.

Question.24. pH of sodium carbonate solution would be less than 7 or more than 7.

Answer. More than 7 because sodium carbonate, being a salt of strong base and weak acid, gives alkaline solution due to hydrolysis.

Question.25. Explain why pH of 0.1 M solution of HCl is same as that of 0.05 M H$_2$SO$_4$.

Answer. HCl and H$_2$SO$_4$ are strong acids and are completely ionised in aqueous solution 0.1 M HCl and 0.05 M H$_2$SO$_4$ produce almost same cone, of H$_3$O$^+$ (aq) on ionisation and hence have practically equal pH. (Note that 1 molecule of H$_2$SO$_4$ gives 2H$_3$O$^+$ ions on ionisation).

CHEMICAL EQUILIBRIUM

EFFECT OF CHANGE OF CONCENTRATION ON CHEMICAL EQUILIBRIUM

It is a common observation that many physical processes and chemical reactions exist in the state of equilibrium. Our focus being on chemical reactions, the answer to Question as to why many chemical reactions do not proceed to completion is that after some time the rates of forward reaction and backward reaction balance each other. This is the state of chemical equilibrium. Applying law of mass action to a reversible reaction,

$$A + B \rightleftharpoons C + D$$

According to the law of mass action, rate of forward reaction, r_1, will be directly proportional to the product of concentrations of A and B and the rate of backward reaction, r_2, will be directly proportional to the products of concentrations of C and D.

Thus, $r_1 = k_1[A][B]$ and $r_2 = k_2[C][D]$

where k_1 and k_2 are the rate constants for the forward and the backward reactions respectively and [A], [B], [C] and [D] are the molar concentrations of A, B, C and D respectively.

At equilibrium, r1 will be equal to r_2

$k_1[A][B] = k_2[C][D]$

$$\frac{k_1}{k_2} = \frac{[C][D]}{[A][B]}$$

Putting $k_2 = Kc$ we have

$$K_c = \frac{[C]^c[D]^d}{[A]^a[B]^b}$$

Kc is called equilibrium constant. Its value is independent of initial concentration of reactants and is a function of temperature but remains constant at a constant temperature. At a given temperature, if the concentration of anyone of the reactants or products is changed, then equilibrium is disturbed and according to Le Chatelier principle, reaction proceeds in that direction which counteracts the change in concentration, so as to maintain the equilibrium. The combined constant k is called equilibrium constant and has a constant value of a reaction at a given temperature. The above equation is known as law of chemical equilibrium

AIM

To study the effect of concentration on the equilibrium between ferric ions and thiocyanate ions.

MATERIAL REQUIRED

Test tubes, test tube stand, droppers, glass rod, beakers, weight box, measuring flask and measuring cylinders. Ferric chloride (0.1 M), potassium thiocyanate (0.1 M) and potassium chloride (0.1 M).

THEORY

When a system in equilibrium is suddenly disturbed, it will respond in some way until equilibrium is re-established. Consider the equilibrium between ferric ions and thiocyanate ions:

$$Fe^{3+}(aq) + SCN^-(aq) \rightleftharpoons [Fe(SCN)^{2+}(aq)]$$

$$\text{pale yellow} \qquad \text{colorless} \qquad \text{deep red}$$

The equilibrium constant for the above reaction can be written as:

$$K = \frac{[Fe(SCN)]^{2+}}{[Fe^{3+}][SCN^-]}$$

Where, $[Fe(SCN)]^{2+}$, $[Fe^{3+}]$ and $[SCN^-]$ are the equilibrium concentrations of the respective species while K is the equilibrium constant. For a particular reaction the value of K is constant at a particular temperature. When concentration of any species involved in the equilibrium is disturbed, the concentration quotient,

$$\frac{[Fe(SCN)]^{2+}}{[Fe^{3+}][SCN^-]}$$

remains no longer equal to K. In order to re-establish the equilibrium, the ions interact in such a way so that the concentration quotient again becomes equal to the equilibrium constant K.

A. EFFECT OF INCREASING CONCENTRATION OF FERRIC IONS

When ferric chloride solution is added to the red solution containing ferric ions, thiocyanate ions and ferric-thiocyanate complex, concentration of ferric ions increases and therefore, the concentration of thiocyanate ions should decrease or that of $[Fe(SCN)]^{2+}$ should increase so as to keep concentration quotient equal to equilibrium constant at a given temperature. Therefore, increase in concentration of ferric ions results in more of thiocyanate ions combining with ferric ions to give more of $[Fe(SCN)]^{2+}$ complex and therefore, the color intensity of red-solution increases. Thus, increase in concentration of Fe^{3+} ions shift the above equilibrium in the forward direction.

B. EFFECT OF INCREASING CONCENTRATION OF THIOCYANATE IONS

Since thiocyanate ion is in the denominator in the equilibrium law equation, the addition of more and more of thiocyanate results in more of ferric ions reacting with thiocyanate ions to give more of $[Fe(SCN)]^{2+}$ complex. Hence, the color intensity of red-solution increases. Thus, increase in the concentration of SCN^- ions shift the above equilibrium in the forward direction.

C. EFFECT OF INCREASING THE CONCENTRATION OF POTASSIUM IONS

When potassium chloride is added to the red solution, concentration of K^+ ions increase. It affects the equilibrium between potassium and thiocyanate ions.

$$KCNS \rightleftharpoons K^+ + SCN^-$$
$$KCl \longrightarrow K^+ + Cl^-$$

Increase in concentration of K^+ ions shift the equilibrium in the backward direction. This results in decrease in concentration of SCN^- ions which in turn shifts the equilibrium (7.2) in the backward direction. In other words, some of the $[Fe(SCN)]^{2+}$ complex dissociates to give Fe^{3+} ions and SCN^- ions. Due to decrease in concentration of $[Fe(SCN)]^{2+}$ the intensity of red color decreases. Thus, increase in concentration of K^+ ions shift the above equilibrium in the backward direction.

PROCEDURE

1. Take a 250 ml beaker thoroughly washed and clean.
2. Put 10 ml of 0.1 M $FeCl_3$ solution in it by using a measuring cylinder.
3. Add 10 ml of 0.1 M KSCN solution with the help of measuring cylinder.
4. A deep red color is obtained due to complex formation $[Fe(SCN)]^{2+}$ (aq).
5. Dilute the above deep red solution by adding 50 ml of distilled water.
6. Take four test tubes and label them as A, B, C and D. Add 10 ml of the deep red solution to each of the four test-tubes.
7. Arrange the test tubes in a test tube stand [Fig. 7.1].

8. Add 5 ml of distilled water to test tube A; 5 ml of 0.1M FeCl₃ solution to test tube B; 5 ml of 0.1 M KSCN solution to test tube C and 5 ml of 0.1 M KCl solution to test tube D.

9. Shake all the tubes well.

10. Now compare the intensity of the colors in test tubes, B, C and D with the red color in test tube A taken as reference tube.

11. The intensity of the red color corresponds to concentration of complex $[Fe(SCN)]^{2+}$ and if the concentration of this ion increases, the color intensity will also increase.

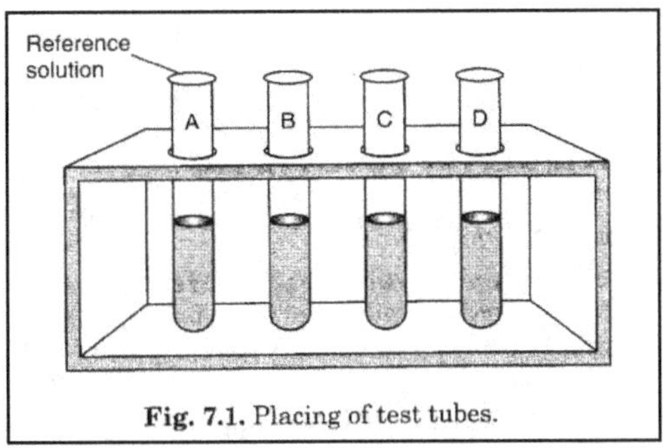

Fig. 7.1. Placing of test tubes.

OBSERVATION

Test tube	Substance added at equilibrium	Change in color	Effect on the concentration of $[Fe(SCN)]^{2+}$	Shift of equilibrium
A	5 ml of water	Reference color	—	—
B	5 ml of 0.1 M FeCl₃ solution	Color deepens	Increases	Towards right
C	5 ml of 0.1 M KSCN solution	Color deepens	Increases	Towards right
D	5 ml of 0.1 M KC₁ solution	Color becomes lighter	Decreases	Towards left

CONCLUSION

Increase in concentration of either of the reactants (Fe^{3+} ions or SCN^- ions) shifts the equilibrium in the forward direction (**towards right**), on the other hand decrease in concentration of any of the reactants shifts the equilibrium in the backward direction (**towards left**).

PRECAUTION

1. Use tubes of almost identical diameter.
2. Dilute solutions of thiocyanate should be used.
3. The intensity of color of a solution should be compared by keeping it and reference side by side and then observing from top.

AIM

Study of the shift in equilibrium in the reaction between $[Co(H_2O)_6]^{2+}$ and Cl^- ions, by changing the concentration of any one of these ions.

THEORY

Following displacement, takes place in the chemical reaction between $[Co(H_2O)_6]^{2+}$ and chloride.

$$[Co(H_2O)_6]^{2+} + 4Cl^- \;\rightleftharpoons\; [CoCl_4]^{2-} + 6H_2O$$

Pink   Blue   equation. (i)

The equilibrium constant is given by the formula:

$$K_c = \frac{[C][D]}{[A][B]}$$

Finding equilibrium constant for the reaction between $[Co(H_2O)_6]^{2+}$ and chloride ions is given by:

$$K = \frac{[[CoCl_4]^{2-}]}{[[Co(H_2O)_6]^{2+}][Cl^-]^4}$$

This reaction takes place in an aqueous medium the concentration of H_2O remains constant.

At equilibrium either $[Co(H_2O)_6]^{2+}$ ion or Cl^- ions concentration is increased, and this would result in an increase in $[CoCl_4]^{2-}$ ion concentration thus, maintaining the value of K as constant. There is a shift in the equilibrium in the forward direction along with the change in color.

The effect of change in concentration of various ions can be study as per Le Chatelier's Principle.

A. EFFECT OF INCREASING CONCENTRATION OF Cl⁻ IONS

On adding water molecules to the blue solution i.e., on increasing the concentration of water molecules for equation. (i) the equilibrium gets shifted to the left side and the concentration of $[Co (H_2O)_6]^{2+}$ increases.so thereby the intensity of blue color decreases and intensity of pink color increases.

$$[Co(H_2O)_6]^{2+} + 4Cl^- \quad [CoCl_4]^{2-} + 6H_2O$$
$$\text{Pink} \qquad\qquad\qquad \text{Blue}$$

B. EFFECT OF INCREASING CONCENTRATION OF WATER MOLECULES

When water is added to the blue solution, more concentration of water (one of the product), shifts the equilibrium to left and conc. of $Co(H_2O)_6]^{2+}$ increases and intensify of blue color decreases or that of pink color increases.

MATERIAL REQUIRED

Conical flask (100 ml), Beakers (100 ml), Burettes, Test tubes, Test tube stand, Glass rod, Acetone/alcohol 60 ml, Concentrated hydrochloric acid 30 ml, Cobalt chloride.

PROCEDURE

1. Take 60 ml of acetone in a 100 ml conical flask and dissolve 0.6000 g $CoCl_2$ in it to get a blue solution.
2. Take 5 test tubes of same size and mark them as A, B, C, D and E.
3. Add 3.0 ml of cobalt chloride solution in each of the test tubes from 'A' to 'E' respectively.
4. Now add 1.0 ml, 0.8 ml, 0.6 ml, 0.4 ml and 0.2 ml of acetone respectively in these test tubes. Add 0.2 ml, 0.4 ml, 0.6 ml and 0.8 ml of water to test tubes B, C, D and E respectively, so that the total volume of solution in each of the test tubes is 4.0 ml.
5. Note the gradual change in color of the mixture from blue to pink with an increase in the amount of water.
6. Take 10 ml cobalt chloride solution in acetone prepared above and add 5 ml distilled water to it. A solution of pink color will be obtained.
7. Take 1.5 ml of pink solution from step (4) in five different test tubes labeled as A′ B′, C′, D′ and E′. Add 2.0 ml, 1.5 ml, 1.0 ml and 0.5 ml of water to the test tubes labelled from A′ to D′ and 0.5 ml, 1.0 ml, 1.5 ml, 2.0 ml and 2.5 ml concentrated HCl respectively in the test tubes A′ to E′ so that total volume of solution in the test tubes is 4 ml.
8. Note the gradual change in color of pink solution to light blue with increasing amounts of hydrochloric acid. Record your observations in tabular form.

OBSERVATION

S. No.	Test tube	Volume of acetone	Volume of cocl₂ sol.	Volume of water added	Color of mixture
1	1	1.0	3.0	0.0	
2	2	0.8	3.0	0.2	
3	3	0.6	3.0	0.4	
4	4	0.4	3.0	0.6	
5	5	0.2	3.0	0.8	

S. No.	Test tube	Volume of conc. HCl added	Volume of aqua complex solution added	Volume of water added	Color of mixture
1	1	0.5	1.5	2.0	
2	2	1.0	1.5	1.5	
3	3	1.5	1.5	1.0	
4	4	2.0	1.5	0.5	
5	5	2.5	1.5	0.0	

RESULT

Increase in the concentration of chloride ions shift the equilibrium to the right and therefore, intensity of blue color increases because of the increase in $[CoCl_4]^{2-}$ ion concentration.

Increase in water concentration shifts the equilibrium to the left and therefore intensity of blue color decreases or of pink color increases because of the increase in $Co(H_2O)_6]^{2+}$ ions concentration.

PRECAUTIONS

1. Use tubes of almost identical diameter.
2. Dilute solutions of thiocyanate should be used.
3. The intensity of color of a solution should be compared by keeping it and reference side by side and then observing from to

Question.1. What is law of mass action?
Answer. The rate at which a chemical substance reacts is directly proportional to its molar concentration. The rate of reaction is directly proportional to the product of the molar concentrations of the reacting substances.

Question. 2. Define reversible reaction?
Answer. The reaction in which the products formed react back to give the reactant molecules are called reversible reactions.

Question.3. What is chemical equilibrium?
Answer. In a chemical reaction when the rate of the forward reaction becomes equal to the rate of the backward reaction, that state is known as chemical equilibrium.

Question.4. State the law of chemical equilibrium.
Answer. For a reversible reaction in equilibrium, the product of the molar concentration of products, divided by the product of the molar concentrations of the reactants, each concentration raised to the power equal to its coefficients is constant at a particular temperature. This constant is called equilibrium constant.

Question.5. How does concentration of reactants affect the equilibrium?
Answer. If the concentration of any of the reactants is increased, the equilibrium shifts in the forward direction.

Question.6. What is the meaning of the statement "the chemical equilibrium is dynamic"?
Answer. Attainment of equilibrium in a chemical reaction does not mean that the reaction has stopped. The reaction is still in progress but the number of moles of the reactants combining in a given time is exactly the same as the number of moles of the reactants produced during the same time in the reverse reaction. Thus, the equilibrium is dynamic in nature and not static.

Question.7. Does the constancy of color intensity indicate the dynamic nature of equilibrium? Explain your answer with appropriate reasons.
Answer. No, because the color would become constant even if the reaction stops altogether at equilibrium.

Question.8. Does temperature affect the equilibrium?
Answer. Yes.

Question.9. What will be effect of increasing the temperature of the reaction mixture at equilibrium?
Answer. On increasing the temperature, the equilibrium shifts in favor of endothermic direction.

Question.10. What is the color of $[Co(H_2O)_6]^{2+}$ ions?
Answer. Pink.

Question.11. What is the formula of the complex ion formed when a solution containing $[Co(H_2O)_6]^{2+}$ ions is treated with hydrochloric acid?
Answer. $[CoCl_4]^{2-}$.

Question.12. What is the color of $[CoCl_4]^{2-}$ ions?

Answer. Blue.

Question.13. What do you understand by a reaction at equilibrium?
Answer. For a reversible reaction, when the rate of forward reaction becomes equal to the rate of backward reaction, the reaction is said to be in the state of equilibrium.

Question.14. What is a reversible reaction?
Answer. A reaction in which the products can react to give back the reactants is called a reversible reaction.

Question.15. What is dynamic equilibrium?
Answer. Any chemical equilibrium is said to be dynamic in nature, since at equilibrium, the reaction is still on at the molecular level. It is just that the rate of forward and backward reaction is same and the reaction appears to be stopped.

Question.16. What is the law of mass action?
Answer. The law of mass action states that the rate of a chemical reaction at any particular temperature is proportional to the product of the molar concentrations of reactants with each concentration term raised to the power equal to the number of molecules of respective reactants taking part in the reaction

Question.17. What is law of equilibrium?
Answer. For a reversible reaction, the rate at which reactants combine at equilibrium is proportional to the products of the equilibrium concentrations raised to their coefficient in the balanced equation and hence for the reaction.

$$aA + bB \rightleftharpoons cC + dD$$

Equilibrium constant, $K = \dfrac{[C]^c[D]^d}{[A]^a[B]^b}$

Question.18. What is the difference between reaction quotient Q and equilibrium constant K?
Answer. The concentration ratio i.e., ratio of product of concentration of products to that of reactants, raised to the power the stoichiometric coefficients is called concentration quotient or reaction quotient. When the reaction quotient denotes the concentrations at equilibrium, it is called equilibrium constant.

Question.19. Give an example of a reversible reaction.
Answer. $N_2(g) + 3H_2(g) \rightleftharpoons 2NH_3(g)$.

Question.20. Define equilibrium constant.
Answer. It is the ratio of the equilibrium concentrations of the products to the equilibrium concentrations of the reactants raised to the power of their stoichiometric coefficients.

Question.21. Define Le Chatelier's principle.
Answer. It states that when a reaction at equilibrium is subjected to any change of concentration, temperature or pressure; the equilibrium shifts in such a way so as to tend to cancel the effect of the change.

Question.22. What is active mass?
Answer. Active mass is molar concentration of the reacting species.

Question.23. What happens to the equilibrium when concentration of any reactant is increased in a reaction mixture at equilibrium?
Answer. When concentration of a reactant is increased in a reaction at equilibrium, the equilibrium shifts in the forward direction.

Question.24. Name the complex formed by adding thiocyanate ions into ferric salt solution.
Answer. Tri Thiocyanate iron (III)

Question.25. How does the equilibrium constant change when ferric ions are added to thiocyanatoiron (III) complex solution?
Answer. Value of equilibrium constant remains same at a given temperature but the concentrations of various species change.

Question.26. When HCl is added to cobalt nitrate solution, which complex is formed?
Answer. A complex compound $[CoCl_4]^{2-}$ is formed. It's name is tetrachlorocobaltate (II) ion.

QUANTITATIVE ANALYSIS (TITRIMETRIC ANALYSIS)

In volumetric analysis, the quantities of the constituents present in the given unknown solution are determined by measuring the volumes of the solutions taking part in the given chemical reaction. The main process of this analysis is called titration which means the determination of the volume of a reagent required to bring a definite reaction to completion. During volumetric analysis we have to prepare solutions of known concentrations. In this chapter we shall study how to prepare solutions of substances with known concentrations. We shall also learn about the process of titration.

CHEMICAL BALANCE

The balance is the principal instrument used in quantitative analysis. One of the most important requirements in quantitative analysis is a sufficiently high degree of precision. The analytical balance used in quantitative macroanalysis can be used for weighing objects not heavier than 100-200 g to a precision of 0.0002 g, i.e., 0.2 mg. The most usual design of a balance of this type is shown in Fig. 8.1.

The most important part, the beam, has three knife edges made of agate or very hard steel [Fig. 8.2. (a)]. The central knife edge rests on a special very smooth agate plate on the top of the balance column. The balance pans are suspended from the terminal knife edges by means of stirrups [Fig. 8.2 (6)].

A pointer is fixed to the center of the beam; as the balance swings the lower end of the pointer moves along the scale, at the bottom of the column. All the three knife edges must be strictly parallel and in the same plane for correct operation of the balance. The knife edges and plates gradually wear out and the balance becomes less precise. To reduce wear and tear as much as possible the balance is provided with an arrest device whereby the balance beam can be raised and the balance "arrested". The balance must be arrested when not in use.

The balance is enclosed in a glass case which protects it from dust, air movements, the operator's breath etc.

The base of the balance rests on screws 1 (Fig. 8.1), whereby the knife edges and agate plates on which they rest are brought into horizontal position by means of a plumb bob attached to the balance column (at the back).

The balance pans 7 are made of some light metal which is nickel-plated or coated with gold or platinum to prevent oxidation. Obviously, substances should never be put directly on the balance pans because this spoils the balance. Therefore, substances are weighed either in special weighing bottles with ground-glass lids [Fig. 8.3 (a)] or on watch glasses [Fig. 8.3 (6)] or in crucibles, test tubes etc.

For the results of weighing to be accurate the weighed object must be of the same temperature as the balance. If a hotter (or colder) object is placed on a balance pan, this has the effect of lengthening (or shortening) the corresponding arm of the beam resulting in incorrect readings.

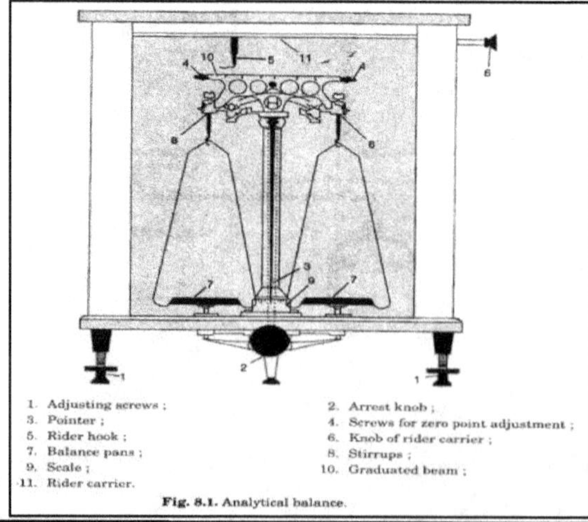

1. Adjusting screws ;	2. Arrest knob ;
3. Pointer ;	4. Screws for zero point adjustment ;
5. Rider hook ;	6. Knob of rider carrier ;
7. Balance pans ;	8. Stirrups ;
9. Scale ;	10. Graduated beam ;
11. Rider carrier.	

Fig. 8.1. Analytical balance.

The weights used with analytical balance are contained in a special box as shown in Fig. 8.4.
Box also contains a pair of forceps for lifting the weights and putting them on and off the balance answer. The forceps should be ivory tipped. The weights must never be touched by hand.

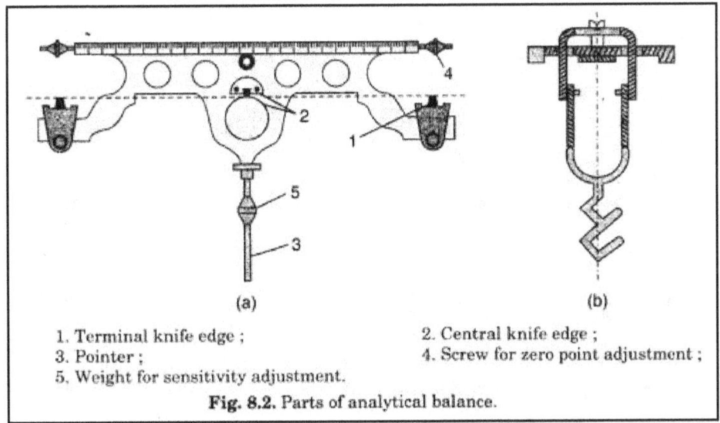

1. Terminal knife edge ;
3. Pointer ;
5. Weight for sensitivity adjustment.

2. Central knife edge ;
4. Screw for zero point adjustment ;

Fig. 8.2. Parts of analytical balance.

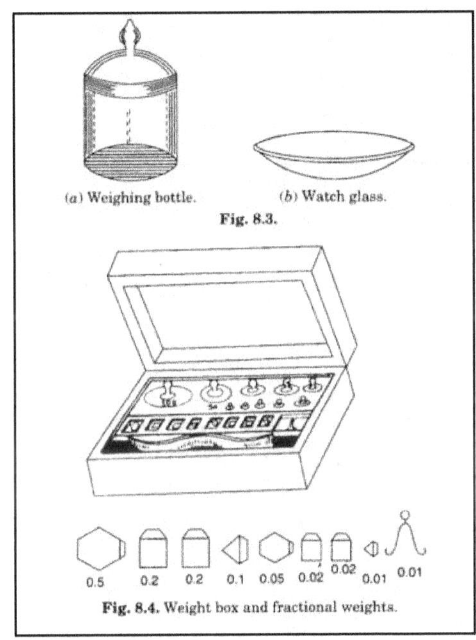

Fig. 8.3.

Fig. 8.4. Weight box and fractional weights.

The weights are coated with gold or platinum to prevent corrosion and consequent changes of weight. The small weights (fractions of a gram) are made of some metal which is not corroded in air, e.g., aluminum or platinum.

The weights are arranged in the box in definite order. There are two usual systems corresponding to the numbers 5:2:2:1 or 5:2:1:1. In accordance with the first system, the box would contain weights of 50, 20, 20, 10, 5, 2, 2, 1 g and in accordance with the second, weights of 50,20,10,10,10, 5, 2,1,1,1 g. Fractions of a gram follow the same systems and are made of different shapes so that small weights are easier to distinguish. For example, frac-tonal weights of 0.5 and 0.05 g are made in shape of regular hexagon, weights 0.2 and 0.02 g are squares and weights 0.1 and 0.01 g are triangles. Each fractional weight has an edge bent at right angle by which it is lifted with the forceps.

By means of the weights an object can be weighed to an accuracy of 0.01 g. Thousandth and ten-thousandth fractions of a gram are weighed by means of the so-called rider. The rider, as shown in Fig. 8.5, is a thin bent wire (usually of aluminum) weighing 0.01 g or 0.005 g, it is attached with the aid of the forceps by its loop on hooks. This hook is fixed to the horizontal rod 11 with the knob 6 outside the balance case. This rod is rotated or moved to place the rider at any desired point on the beam. The beam has a scale 10 the graduations of which differ in different balances. If the rider is moved from the zero division to the fifth (inexactly over the central knife edge), this is equivalent to removal of 0.005 g from the left-hand pan or a similar increase of the load on the right-hand pan.

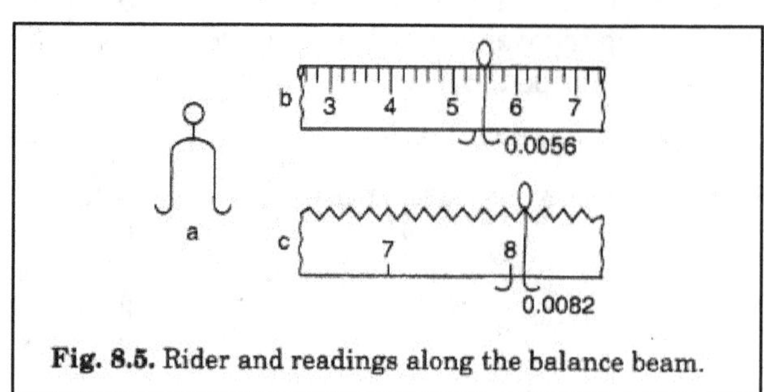

Fig. 8.5. Rider and readings along the balance beam.

SETTING THE BALANCE

Before the substance can be weighed in a balance it has to be first set in proper order. The following steps are followed for setting the balance:

1. Clean the pans of the balance with a hairbrush or a clean handkerchief.
2. Level the balance by adjusting the levelling screws. See that the pointer rests at zero. Close the front door of the balance.
3. Now rotate the key arrest knob to raise the beam and see that the pointer swings or oscillates equal divisions on both sides of the zero mark as shown in Fig. 8.6. If it does not oscillate equally on both the sides arrest the beam and move the adjusting screws (4) till on rotating the arrest knob, the pointer oscillates equally on both sides of the zero mark. Again, arrest the beam.

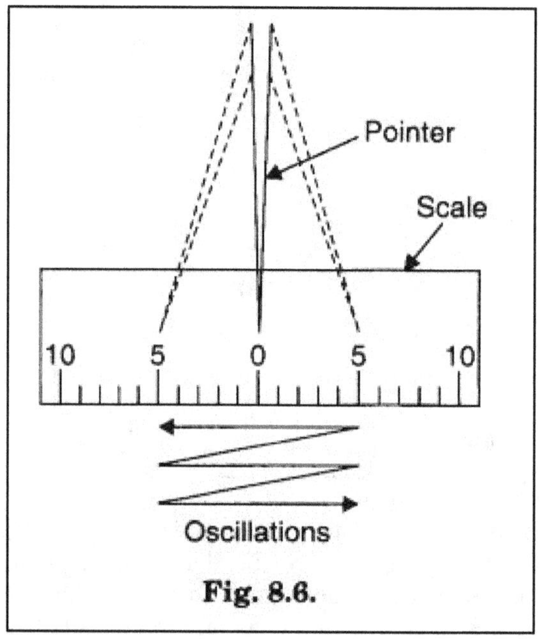

Fig. 8.6.

WEIGHING THE SUBSTANCE

1. Take a clean and dry watch glass or weighing bottle and place it carefully on the left-hand pan of the balance.
2. Pick out an appropriate gram weight from the weight box with the help of forceps and place it on the right-hand pan. If the gram weight is heavier as compared to the weight of the watch glass, remove it and try lower weight. The gram weight should be slightly less than the weight of the watch glass (less than 1 gram).
3. After placing the correct gram weight start placing fractional weights.
4. Use rider for weights lighter than 10 mg.
5. Record the correct weight of empty watch glass.
6. Now add weights (gram weights and fractional weights), equal to the amount of the substance to be taken, in the right-hand pan.

7. Now add required quantity of the substance to be weighed on the watch glass.
8. Take out the watch glass along with the substance.
9. Clean the balance and close it.

PRECAUTIONS FOR HANDLING THE ANALYTICAL BALANCE

In weighing it must be remembered that the analytical balance is a precise physical instrument which must be handled with great care.

To avoid damage to the balance and to ensure accurate weighing the following rules must be strictly observed:

1. Check the state of the balance before each weighing. Remove dust from the pans with a soft brush and find the zero point of the balance.
2. The unrested balance must not be touched. The balance must be arrested before the object and weights are put on the pans or taken off them. The balance must be arrested before the rider is moved along the beam; The knob must be turned slowly and carefully.
3. Do not move the balance from its place.
4. Never overload the balance above the permitted load (usually 100g) as this causes damage.
5. Do not place wet or dirty objects on the balance. Do not spill anything inside the balance case.

SOME IMPORTANT TERMS

1. STANDARD SOLUTION

A solution whose concentration is known is called a standard solution.

Concentration of a solution is generally expressed as normality or molarity.

2. NORMALITY

Normality of a solution is defined as the number of gram-equivalents of solute per liter of solution. It is denoted by N.

$$\text{Normality} = \frac{\text{Number of gram-equivalents of solute}}{\text{Volume of solution (L)}}$$

$$= \frac{\text{Mass of solute (in grams) per liter of solution}}{\text{Gram - equivalent mass of the solute}}$$

$$\therefore \text{ Number of gram equivalents of solute} = \text{Normality} \times \text{Volume of solution (L)}.$$

A solution containing one gram-equivalent of solute per liter of solution is called normal solution.

Equivalent mass of a substance can be obtained from its molecular mass.

Equivalent mass of an acid is defined as the mass of the acid which can furnish one mole of hydrogen ions.

$$\text{Equivalent mass of an acid} = \frac{\text{Molecular mass of acid}}{\text{Number of available hydrogen ions per molecule}}$$

$$= \frac{\text{Molecular mass of acid}}{\text{Basicity of acid}}$$

Similarly, equivalent mass of a base is defined as the mass of the base which can furnish one mole of hydroxyl ions. It may also be defined as the mass of the base which is completely neutralized by one equivalent of the acid.

$$\text{Equivalent mass of a base} = \frac{\text{Molecular mass of base}}{\text{Number of hydroxylions per molecule}}$$

$$= \frac{\text{Molecular mass of base}}{\text{Acidity of base}}$$

In case of salts,

$$\text{Equivalent mass of a salt} = \frac{\text{Molecular or formula mass of salt}}{\text{Total valency of metal ion in the formula unit}}$$

Equivalent masses of some compounds (acids, bases and salts) are given in Table 8.1.

Table 8.1. Equivalent Masses of Some Compounds

Name of Compound	Formula	Molecular Mass	Equivalent Mass
1. Hydrochloric acid	HCl	36.5	36.5
2. Sulfuric acid	H_2SO_4	98	49
3. Acetic acid	CH_3COOH	60	60
4. Oxalic acid	COOH $2H_2O$ COOH	126	63
5. Sodium hydroxide	NaOH	40	40
6. Sodium carbonate	Na_2CO_3	106	53
7. Sodium bicarbonate	$NaHCO_3$	84	84

3. MOLARITY

Molarity of a solution may be defined as the number of gram moles of solute per liter of the solution. It is denoted by M. Mathematically; it may be expressed as:

$$\text{Molarity} = \frac{\text{Gram moles of solute}}{\text{Volume of solution (L)}}$$

$$= \frac{\text{Mass of solute (in grams) per liter of solution}}{\text{Molar mass of the solute}}$$

Gram moles of solute = Molarity × Volume of solution (L)

A solution containing one gram mole of solute per liter of solution is called molar solution.

PREPARING A STANDARD SOLUTION

A standard solution is prepared by dissolving a definite weight of substance (a primary standard), in solvent to prepare a definite volume of solution. A substance is classified as a primary standard if it has following characteristics:

1. It is easily available in state of high purity.
2. It is neither hygroscopic nor deliquescent.
3.   It shows high solubility in water.
4. It does not dissociate or decompose during storage.
5. It should react with another substance instantaneously and in stoichiometric proportion.

Oxalic acid, Mohr's salt, potassium dichromate and sodium thiosulphate are some examples of primary standards. Substances whose standard solutions cannot be prepared directly are called **Secondary standards**. For example, potassium permanganate, sodium hydroxide and potassium hydroxide. A secondary standard cannot be used for preparing a standard solution by direct weighing.

APPARATUS USED IN VOLUMETRIC ANALYSIS

In volumetric analysis, the volumes of the various solutions should be measured accurately. The apparatus required is as follows:

i. Graduated-burette, pipette, measuring flasks and measuring cylinders.
ii. General titration flasks, beaker, tile, glass-rod, funnel, weighing bottle, wash bottle.

BURETTE

It is a long, cylindrical tube of uniform bore fused at the lower end with a stop cock (Fig. 8.8). It is graduated in milliliters from 0 to 50. Each division is further sub-divided into ten equal parts. Therefore, each sub-division reads 0.1 ml.

Before a burette is filled with the solution, it is thoroughly washed, so that no greasy matter remains sticking inside or outside the burette. Take a small volume of solution (to be taken in it as titrant), close the upper mouth of the burette

with the thumb and hold in horizontal position as shown in Fig. 8.10. Rotate the burette so as to wet the inner walls of the burette. Reject this solution through the stop-cock. This process is known as rinsing. Then the burette is filled through a funnel inserted in the top Fig. 8.9. The funnel must then be taken out after filling the burette.

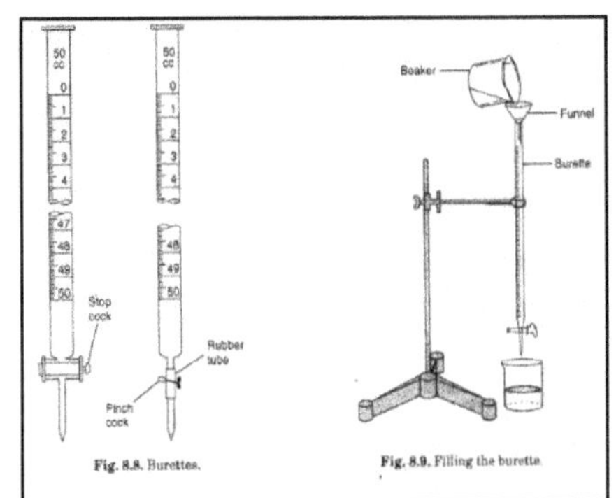

Fig. 8.8. Burettes.

Fig. 8.9. Filling the burette.

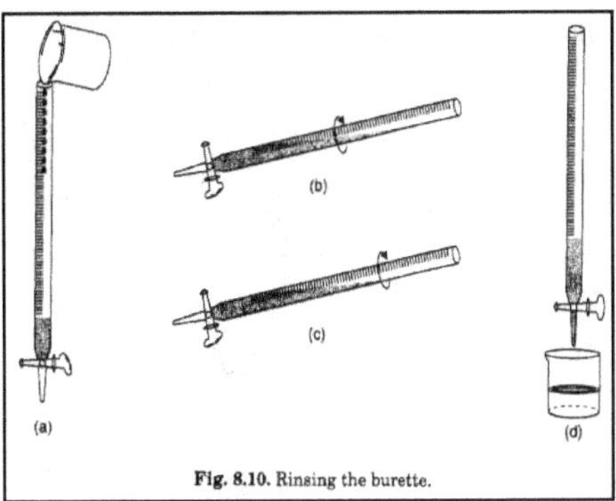

Fig. 8.10. Rinsing the burette.

Care must be taken that no air bubbles remain in the narrow bottom tip of the burette. To remove this air, the stop-cock is opened and the liquid is allowed to run out rapidly into the beaker or flask.Burette reading forms the most important aspect of the experiment, therefore, burette should be read very carefully, after removing parallax.To read the burette, hold behind the level of the liquid and in contact with the burette a piece of white paper to illuminate the surface of the liquid. This paper, called anti-parallax card, eliminates errors in reading due to parallax. In order to prepare an anti-parallax card, take a rectangular piece of paper and fold it half. Give two cuts as shown in Fig. 8.11. Open the fold and mount it on the burette.

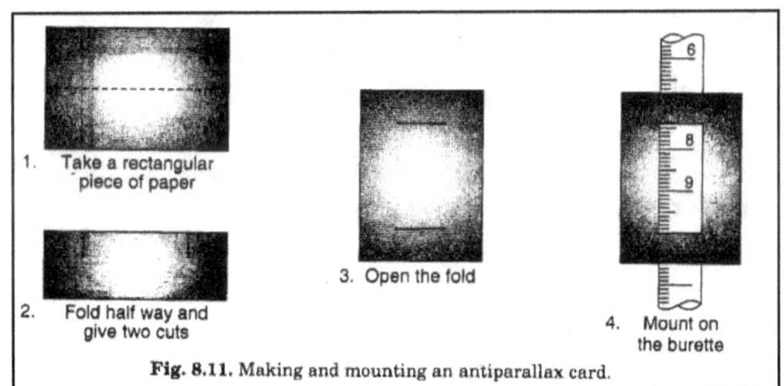

Fig. 8.11. Making and mounting an antiparallax card.

It is to be remembered that in case of colorless solutions lower meniscus is read while in case of colored solutions, level is read from the upper meniscus. This is due to the reason that in case of colored solutions lower meniscus is not clearly visible.

Placing your eye exactly in front of meniscus (Fig. 8.13) of the solution take initial reading and then final reading at the end. Find out the difference between two readings to obtain the volume of solution consumed.

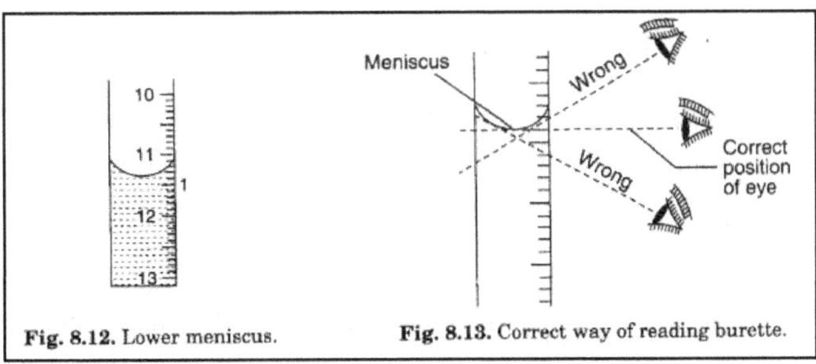

Fig. 8.12. Lower meniscus.

Fig. 8.13. Correct way of reading burette.

PRECAUTION

1. See that stop-cock does not leak.
2. Remove the funnel immediately after filling the burette.
3. Do not allow any air bubble to remain inside the burette.
4. Always use anti-parallax card and place the eye exactly in the level of meniscus.
5. Let no drops of solution be hanging at the tip of the burette at the end point.

PIPETTE

This is a small and handy apparatus used for accurate measurements of definite volume of solution. It consists of a long narrow tube with cylindrical bulb in the middle and a jet at its lower end.

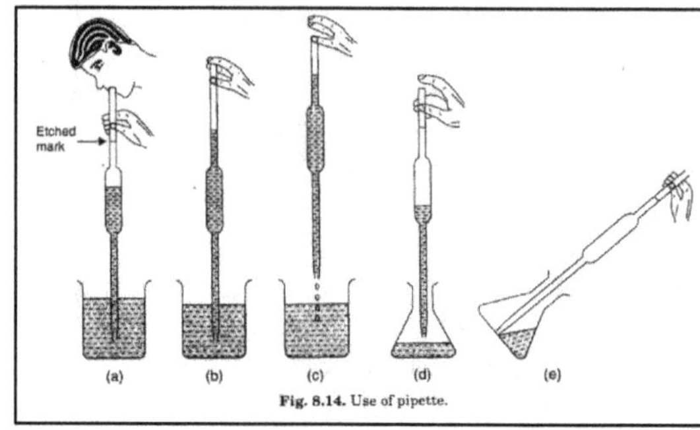

Fig. 8.14. Use of pipette.

On the upper part of the stem, there is an etched circular mark. On the bulb is marked the volume which the pipette can deliver when filled up to the circular mark [Fig. 8.14 (a)].

Before a pipette is filled with the solution, it is washed thoroughly and rinsed. The upper part of pipette is then held by the thumb and middle finger of the right hand, the lower end is dipped into the liquid and the solution is sucked into the pipette until the liquid level is about 2 cm above the mark. The open end of pipette is then closed with index finger. The liquid is allowed to run slowly until the lower edge of meniscus just touches the mark. The solution is then allowed to run freely out of the pipette [Fig. 8.14 (d)] When no more of the liquid flows out, touch the tip of the pipette with the bottom of the flask [Fig. 8.14 (e)]. Some liquid will still remain in the pipette. Do not remove it by blowing because the pipette is calibrated taking this liquid into account.

PRECAUTION

1. Never close the pipette with the thumb.
2. Keep the lower end always dipping in the liquid while sucking the liquid.
3. Never pipette out hot or corrosive solutions.
4. Do not blow out the last drop of the solution from the jet end.

PROCESS OF TITRATION

The process of titration is carried out to find the volume of one solution required to react completely with a certain known volume of solution of some other substance. This is the most important step in volumetric analysis. The process of titration is carried out as under:

1. Place a glazed white tile below the burette and place the titration flask on the glazed tile below the burette nozzle. Adjust the height of the burette so that the nozzle tip just enters the mouth of the titration flask.
2. Note initial reading of the burette after filling it with the solution and run out the solution from the burette (one ml at a time) by opening the stop cock with the left hand. The titration flask is kept in the right hand as shown in Fig. 8.15.
3. Give rotatory motion to the titration flask throughout the titration.
4. Continue running more of the solution from the burette into the titration flask, keeping it all the time shaking. The solution should fall directly into the solution of titration flask. It should not fall on the walls of flask.

5. Stop addition of the solution when the end point is reached and take final reading of the burette. The difference between the final and initial readings gives rough volume of the solution used for completion of the reaction.
6. The solution from the titration flask is thrown away and the titration flask is washed thoroughly first by keeping it under tap water and then with a little of distilled water. Do not rinse the titration flask.
7. Pour more solution in the burette.
8. Pipette out 20 ml of the solution into the titration flask and add 1-2 drops of the indicator solution.

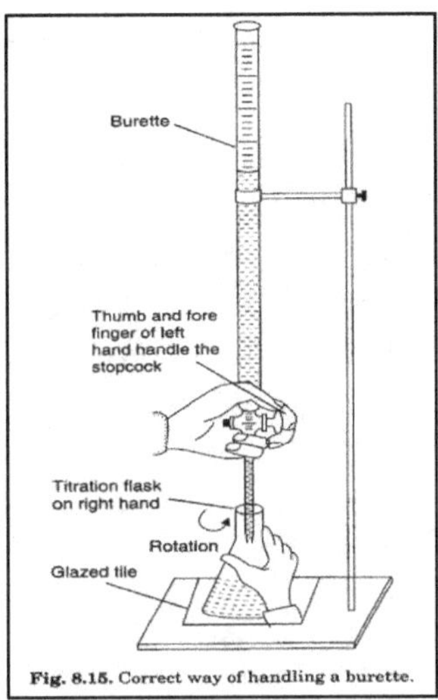

Fig. 8.15. Correct way of handling a burette.

9. Take initial reading of the burette. Run solution from the burette into the titration flask slowly with constant shaking. Continue adding the solution till the volume added is 1 ml less than the rough volume found out in the first titration. Now add solution from the burette dropwise.
10. Continue adding solution dropwise from the burette, till by addition of last single drop, the end point is attained.
11. Note down the final reading of the burette. The difference between the final and initial readings of the burette gives the exact volume of the solution required for completion of the reaction.
12. Check the correctness of the end point by adding one drop of solution (taken in the titration flask) with the help of a pipette. Restoration of original color confirms the correctness of the end point.
13. Perform 5 to 6 titrations so that at least three concordant readings (difference not more than 0.05 ml) are obtained.

Recording of Volumetric Analysis in the Practical Notebook

Left hand page (with pencil)	Right hand page (with ball pen)
Date	Date
Experiment	Experiment
Chemical equation	Requirement
Indicator	Theory
End point	Procedure
Observations	Result
Calculations	General calculations

LAW OF EQUIVALENTS

According to this law, the number of equivalents of the substance to be titrated (titer) is equal to the number of equivalents of the titrant used.

Derivation of the normality equation. Consider an acid-alkali neutralization reaction.

Let V_1 cm^3 of an acid solution of N_1 normality require V_2 cm^3 of base of N_2 normality.

We know that 1000 cm^3 of 1 N acid solution contains acid = 1 gram equivalent.

V_1 cm^3 of 1 N acid contains acid = 11000 × V_1 gm equivalents.

Thus, number of gram equivalents of acid in V_1 cm^3 of N_1 acid solution = $V_1 N_1 1000$

Similarly, number of gram equivalents of base in V_2 cm^3 of its N_2 solution = $V_2 N_2 1000$

By the law of equivalents, at the end point,

$V_1 N_1 1000 = V_2 N_2 1000$

$N_1 V_1 = N_2 V_2$

It is known as normality equation. If three factors (V_1, V_2, N_1) are known, N_2 can be calculated by using above formula. In terms of molarities, we can proceed as [Molarity (M_1) × Volume (V_1)] of Acid [Molarity (M_2) × Volume (V_2)] of Base = Stoichiometric coefficient of the acid in the balanced equation Stoichiometric coefficient of the base in the balance equation

For a reaction between HCl and Na_2CO_3

$$Na_2CO_3 + \underset{\text{2 moles}}{2HCl} \longrightarrow 2NaCl + CO_2 + H_2O$$
$$\underset{\text{1 mole}}{}$$

Thus,

(Molarity × Volume) of HCl (Molarity × Volume) of Na_2CO_3 = 21

ACID-BASE TITRATIONS

In acid-base titrations the amount of the substance is determined by titrating it against a standard solution of acid or base (depending upon the titrant). The chemical reaction involved in acid base titration is called neutralization reaction. Neutralization involves

$$\underset{\text{(Acid)}}{H_3O^+(aq)} + \underset{\text{(Base)}}{OH^-(aq)} \longrightarrow \underset{\text{(Water)}}{H_2O(l)}$$

To know the end point or the neutralization point, an indicator is used.

An **indicator** is a substance whose solution helps in locating the end point by undergoing a color change. Common indicators used are organic compounds.

Indicator	Color in Basle Medium	Color in Acidic Medium
Phenolphthalein	Pink	Colorless
Methyl orange	Yellow	Pink or red

Selection of indicator is made according to the solutions used for titration.

For **strong acid** and **strong alkali** titration **phenolphthalein** is the best choice.

For **strong acid** and **weak alkali** titration **methyl orange** suits the best.

Weak acid and **strong alkali** titrations **phenolphthalein** is most suitable.

AIM

To prepare 250 ml of standard solution of N/10 oxalic acid taking pure crystalline oxalic acid.

MATERIAL REQUIRED

chemical balance, dropper, weight box, weight bottle, measuring flask, funnel

THEORY

Crystalline oxalic acid is a primary standard, its standard solution can be prepared directly.

The formula for crystalline oxalic acid is $COOH - COOH. 2H_2O$. The ionic equation for the oxidation of oxalic acid is:

$$COOH \rightarrow 2CO_2 + 2H^+ + 2e^-$$

It is clear from the above equation that two electrons are given out during oxidation of one molecule of oxalic acid.

Equation. mass of oxalic acid = Mol. mass of oxalic acid / No. of electrons lost by one molecule of it

= 126 / 2 = 63

Strength (g/l) = Normality × Equation. mass

= 1 / 10 × 63 = 6.3 g/l

For preparing 1 liter of N/10 oxalic acid solution 6.3 g of it have to be dissolved.

For preparing 250 ml of N/10 oxalic acid, oxalic acid crystals required

= 6.3/1000 × 250 = 1.575 g.

PROCEDURE

1. Take a watch glass, wash it with distilled water and then dry it.
2. Weigh the clean and dried watch glass accurately and record its weight in the notebook.
3. Weigh 1.575 g oxalic acid on the watch glass accurately and record this weight in the note-book.
4. Transfer gently and carefully the oxalic acid from the watch glass into a clean 250 ml beaker. Wash the watch glass with distilled water with the help of a wash bottle to transfer the particles sticking to it into the beaker. The volume of distilled water for this purpose should not be more than 50 ml.
5. Dissolve oxalic acid crystals in the beaker by gentle stirring with a clean glass rod.
6. When the oxalic acid in the beaker is completely dissolved, transfer carefully the entire solution from the beaker into a 250 ml measuring flask (volumetric flask) with the help of a funnel.
7. Wash the beaker with distilled water. Transfer the washings into the measuring flask.
8. Finally wash the funnel well with distilled water with the help of a wash bottle to transfer the solution sticking to the funnel into the measuring flask.
9. Add enough distilled water to the measuring flask carefully, up to just below the etched mark on it, with the help of a wash bottle.

PRECAUTION
1. Weighing should be done accurately.
2. Use distilled water to prepare solution.
3. Last few drops should be very carefully added using a dropper such that the volume should not exceed the mark.
4. Lower meniscus should be observed since oxalic acid solution is a colorless
5. solution.

Experiment 2

AIM

To prepare 250ml of N/10 sodium carbonate solution

MATERIAL REQUIRED
Anhydrous sodium carbonate and distilled water, chemical balance, dropper, weight box, weighing bottle, measuring flask, funnel

THEORY
$Na_2CO_3(aq) + 2HCl(aq) \longrightarrow 2NaCl(aq) + CO_2(g) + H_2O(l)$

Hence, equivalent mass of $Na_2CO_3 = \dfrac{\text{Molecular mass of } Na_2CO_3}{2} = \dfrac{106}{2} = 53$ g/equiv.

Calculation of amount of sodium carbonate to be weighed (if Normality is given)

$$N = \frac{\text{Wt. in grams}}{\text{Equivalent weight}} \times \frac{1000}{V(\text{ ml})}$$

$$\left(\text{For } \frac{N}{10}, 250 \text{ ml solution}\right) \quad \frac{1}{10} = \frac{\text{Weight}}{53} \times \frac{1000}{250}$$

Weight of Na_2CO_3 to be weighed $= 1.325$ g

Calculation of amount of sodium carbonate be weighed (if Molarity is given)

$$\text{Molarity} = \frac{W_{Na_2CO_3}}{\text{Molecular wt.}} \times \frac{1000}{250}$$

$$\Rightarrow \frac{1}{20} = \frac{W_{Na_2CO_3}}{106} \times \frac{1000}{250}$$

$$\Rightarrow W_{Na_2CO_3} = \frac{106}{20 \times 4} = 1.325 \text{ g}$$

PROCEDURE, RESULT, PRECAUTION
To be followed similar to experiment 1

Experiment 3

AIM

To determine the strength of a given solution of sodium hydroxide by titrating it against a standard solution of N/10 oxalic acid.

MATERIAL REQUIRED

Burette, pipette, conical flask, funnel, N/10 oxalic acid, NaOH solution (approximately N/1O), phenolphthalein.

PROCEDURE

$$\underset{\underset{COOH}{|}}{COOH}(aq) + 2NaOH(aq) \rightarrow \underset{\underset{COONa}{|}}{COONa}\ (aq) + 2H_2O(l)$$

Oxalic acid solution is titrated against NaOH solution using phenolphthalein as indicator.
Oxalic acid is a dibasic acid and sodium hydroxide is a monoacidic base. Hence

$$\text{Equivalent mass of oxalic acid} = \frac{\text{Molecular mass}}{2} = \frac{126}{2} = 63 \text{ g/equiv.}$$

$$\text{Equivalent mass of NaOH} = \frac{\text{Molecular mass}}{1} = \frac{40}{1} = 40 \text{ g/equiv.}$$

1. Rinse and fill the burette with the given sodium hydroxide solution.
2. Rinse the pipette with the oxalic acid solution and pipette out 20 ml of this solution in a washed titration flask.
3. Add 1-2 drops of phenolphthalein indicator to the titration flask.
4. Note the initial reading of the burette and run sodium hydroxide solution slowly in the titration flask till the faint permanent pink color is obtained.
5. Note the final reading of the burette and find out the volume of oxalic acid solution used.
6. Repeat the procedure 4-5 times to get a set of at least three concordant readings.

OBSERVATION

Molarity of NaOH solution = 0.1 M
Volume of oxalic acid solution taken in each titration = 10.0 ml
Indicator = phenolphthalein
End point = colorless to pink

S. No.	Initial reading of the burette	Final reading of the burette	Volume of the sodium hydroxide solution used
1.	—	—	— ml
2.	—	—	— ml
3.	—	—	— ml
4.	—	—	— ml

CALCULATION IN CASE OF NORMALITY GIVEN

$$N_1 V_1 = N_2 V_2 \Rightarrow N_{NaOH} \times V_{NaOH} = N_{oxalic\ acid} \times V_{oxalic\ acid}$$

$$N_{NaOH} = \frac{N_{oxalic\ acid} \times V_{oxalic\ acid}}{V_{NaOH}} = \frac{\frac{1}{10} \times 10}{10.1} = 0.099\ N$$

Strength of NaOH solution $= N_{NaOH} \times$ Equivalent wt. of NaOH $= N_{NaOH} \times 40 = 0.099 \times 40 = 3.96$ g/L

CALCULATION IN CASE MORALITY IS GIVEN

$$n_1 M_1 V_1 = n_2 M_2 V_2$$
$$n_{oxalic\ acid} \times M_{oxalic\ acid} \times V_{oxalic\ acid} = n_{NaOH} \times M_{NaOH} \times V_{NaOH}$$

$$M_{NaOH} = \frac{n_{oxalicacid} \times M_{oxalic\ acid} \times V_{oxalic\ acid}}{n_{NaOH} \times V_{NaOH}} = \frac{2 \times \frac{1}{20} \times 10}{1 \times 10.1} = \frac{1}{10.1} M = 0.099 M$$

Strength of NaOH solution $= M_{NaOH} \times$ Molecular weight $= 0.099 \times 40 = 3.96$ g/L

Since n factor for NaOH Sol is 1 NaOH being monoacidic base, the value of normality of NaOH is equal to its molarity.

RESULT
The strength of given sodium hydroxide is 3.96 g/L

PRECAUTIONS

1. Do not rinse the conical flask.
2. Wash the conical flask with water after each titration.
3. Rinse the burette and pipette with the solution to be taken in it.
4. Note down the lower meniscus of the colorless solution of NaOH and oxalic acid. All the precautions given in the handling of apparatus under 'introduction' of this unit should be observed.

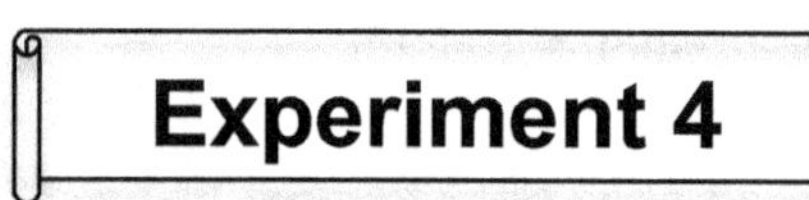

AIM
To determine the strength of a given solution of hydrochloric acid by titrating it against standard N//10 sodium carbonate solution.

MATERIAL REQUIRED
Sodium carbonate solution N/10 OR M/20, Hydrochloric acid (approx. N/10 OR M/20) Methyl orange., burette, pipette, conical flask, funnel.

PROCEDURE
1. The molarity of hydrochloric acid is determined by titrating it against the standard solution of sodium carbonate using methyl orange as indicator.

2. Strength of the acid is determined by multiplying its molarity with its molecular mass which is 36.5

$$Na_2CO_3(aq) + 2HCl(aq) \longrightarrow 2NaCl(aq) + CO_2(g) + H_2O(l)$$

INDICATOR. METHYL ORANGE.
END POINT. YELLOW TO PINK (ACID IN BURETTE).

1. Take a burette and wash it with water.
2. Rinse the burette with the given solution of hydrochloric acid and fill it with it.
3. Rinse the pipette with the given sodium carbonate solution and pipette out 20 ml of this solution in a washed titration flask.
4. Add 2-3 drops of methyl orange indicator to the titration flask and place it just below the nozzle of the burette over a white glazed tile.
5. Note down the initial reading of the burette and run the acid solution slowly and dropwise to the titration flask till the color of the solution changes from yellow to light pink.
6. Note the final reading and find the volume of hydrochloric acid used.
7. Repeat the procedure to take a set of at least three concordant readings.

OBSERVATIONS

Molarity of Na_2CO_3 solution = 0.05 M

Volume of Na_2CO_3 solution taken in each titration = 20.0 ml.

S. No.	Initial reading of the burette	Final reading of the burette	Volume of the sodium hydroxide solution used
1.	—	–	— ml
2.	—	—	— ml
3.	—	—	— ml

CALCULATION

$$N_1 V_1 = N_2 V_2 \text{ or } n_1 M_1 V_1 = n_2 M_2 V_2$$

$$N_{HCl} \times V_{HCl} = N_{Na_2CO_3} \times V_{Na_2CO_3}$$

$$N_{HCl} = \frac{N_{Na_2CO_3} \times V_{Na_2CO_3}}{V_{HCl}} = \frac{0.1 \times 10}{V_{HCl}} = \ldots\ldots. N$$

Strength of HCl solution = $N_{HCl} \times$ Equivalent weight of HCl = $N_{HCl} \times 36.5$ g/L = $\cdots \ldots \ldots$ gL

RESULT

The strength of the given solution of HCl is ………. g/L

PRECAUTION

Same as experiment 3.

Experiment 5

AIM

To determine volumetrically the percentage purity of the given sample of anhydrous sodium carbonate,

6g of which has been dissolved per liter of solution. You are provided with N/10 HCL solution.

MATERIAL REQUIRED
Hydrochloric acid solution N/10, Anhydrous sodium carbonate solution prepared by dissolving 6g of impure compound, burette, pipette, conical flask, funnel.

PROCEDURE
Same as experiment 4

CALCULATION
The time when 6g of impure sample of anhydrous sodium carbonate is dissolved in water to make 1l of solution. The amount of sodium carbonate present in it is less than 6g. When this solution is titrated against standard solution of HCL, the strength of this solution with respect to the amount of sodium carbonate can be calculated.

% purity = calculated strength/ given strength $\times$ 100

Volume of Na_2CO_3 solution in titration flask = 10 ml
Volume of HCl solution used (concordant burette reading) = 10.1 ml (say)

<table>
<tr><td align="center">Using Normality</td><td align="center">Using Molarity</td></tr>
<tr><td align="center">$N_{HCl} \times V_{HCl} = N_{Na_2CO_3} \times V_{Na_2CO_3}$</td><td align="center">$n_{HCl} \times M_{HCl} \times V_{HCl} = n_{Na_2CO_3} \times M_{Na_2CO_3} \times V_{Na_2CO_3}$</td></tr>
<tr><td align="center">$\dfrac{1}{10} \times 10.1 = N_{Na_2CO_3} \times 10$</td><td align="center">$1 \times \dfrac{1}{10} \times 10.1 = 2 \times M_{Na_2CO_3} \times 10$</td></tr>
<tr><td align="center">$N_{Na_2CO_3} = 0.101\ N$</td><td align="center">$M_{Na_2CO_3} = 0.0505M$</td></tr>
</table>

Strength $= N \times$ Equation. wt. $= 0.101 \times 53 = 5.353$ g/L   Strength $= M \times$ Mol wt. $= 0.0505 \times 106 = 5.353$g/L

CALCULATE PERCENTAGE PURITY
% Purity $= \dfrac{\text{Calculated strength (Pure } Na_2CO_3)}{\text{Given strength (Impure } Na_2CO_3)} \times 100 = \dfrac{5.353}{6.0} \times 100 = 89.2\%.$

PRECAUTION
Exactly same as experiment 4

Experiment 6

AIM
To determine volumetrically the number of water molecules of crystallization in oxalic acid

$$\left(\begin{array}{l} COOH \\ | \\ COOH \end{array} .xH_2O \right)$$ **6g of which has been dissolved to make 1L of solution. You are provided with M/10 NaOH solution.**

MATERIAL REQUIRED
Sodium hydroxide solution M/10 hydrated oxalic acid solution, 6g of which has been dissolved to make 1L solution., burette, pipette, conical flask, funnel.

PROCEDURE
Same as experiment 3
The experiment involves the titration between oxalic acid and NaOH solution as explained in experiment number-3. From the concordant burette reading, molarity of oxalic acid can be calculated which further enables us to calculate the

molecular weight of hydrated oxalic acid if the strength is given. Now using the following formula; the number of waters of crystallization can be computed.

FORMULA

Mole mass of hydrated compound = molecular mass of anhydrous compound + 18 × number of H_2O of crystallization

CALCULATION

Volume of oxalic acid in titration flask = 10 ml.

Volume of NaOH solution used (concordant burette reading) = 9.9 ml (say)

$$n_{\text{oxalic acid}} \times M_{\text{oxalic acid}} \times V_{\text{oxalic acid}} = n_{\text{NaOH}} \times M_{\text{NaOH}} \times V_{\text{NaOH}}$$

$$2 \times M_{\text{oxalic acid}} \times 10 = 1 \times \frac{1}{10} \times 9.9$$

$$M_{\text{oxalic acid}} = 0.0495M$$

$$\text{Strength}_{\text{oxalic acid}} = \text{Molarity}_{\text{oxalic acid}} \times \text{Mol, wt. of hydrated oxalic acid}$$

$$6 \text{ (given)} = 0.0495 \times (90 + 18x) \quad (\text{Let } x \text{ be the water of crystallisation})$$

$$6 = 4.455 + 0.891x$$

$$x = \frac{1.545}{0.891} = 1.73 \approx 2$$

i.e., number of water of crystallization of oxalic acid is 2 .

RESULT

Number of water of crystallization of oxalic acid is 2

PRECAUTION

Same as experiment 3

VIVA VOCE 

Question.1. What is the principle of volumetric analysis?
Answer. In volumetric analysis, concentration of a solution is determined by allowing a known volume of a solution to react quantitatively with another solution of known concentration.

Question.2. What is an indicator?
Answer. Substance which changes color when the reaction between two reactants is complete is called an indicator. It gives different colors in different mediums and helps in the detection of the end point.

Question.3. What is an equivalence point?
Answer. The stage of the titration when the reaction is just complete is called equivalence point.

Question.4. What is an end point?
Answer. After the reaction between the substance and the standard solution is practically complete; with one extra drop the indicator shows a clear visual change in the liquid being titrated. The stage in the titration at which this occurs is called the end point.

Question.5. What is a titrant?
Answer. The reagent of known concentration is called titrant.

Question.6. What is a titrant?
Answer. The substance being titrated is called titrant.

Question.7. How are reactions classified in volumetric analysis?
Answer. The reactions employed in titrimetric i.e., volumetric analysis fall into two main classes:
(a) Those in which no change in oxidation state occurs; these are dependent upon the combination of ions. It includes neutralisation (acid-base) reactions, complex formation reactions (EDTA-titrations) and precipitation reactions.
(b) Oxidation-reduction reactions; these involve a change of oxidation state; as redox reaction between $KMnO_4$ & Mohr's salt or Oxalic acid.

Question.8. What is a standard solution?
Answer. A standard solution is one which contains a

known weight of the reagent in a definite volume of solution.

Question.9. Define molarity.
Answer. Molarity is defined as the number of moles of solute present per liter of solution.

$$M = \frac{Wt.}{Molecular\ Wt.} \times \frac{1000}{V(ml)}$$

Question.10. Define normality.
Answer. Normality is defined as the equivalent of solute present in 1L of solution.

$$N = \frac{Wt.}{Equivalent\ Wt.} \times \frac{1000}{V(ml)}$$

Question.11. How are molarity and normality related?
Answer. $N = nM$

used?
Answer. Burette and pipette should be rinsed before use so that any drop of water present in them after washing do not affect the concentration while doing titration.

Question.14. Should a titration flask also be rinsed?
Answer. No, since the rinsing of the titration flask will increase the volume, will make it more than the pipetted one.

Question.15. Why the last drop of the pipette must not be blown out?
Answer. Because the last drop in the jet of the pipette is not counted in the volume of the pipette.

Question.16. Why should pipette not be held from it's bulb?
Answer. Because the heat of the body may expand the glass at the bulb, thereby increasing the volume of the pipette and hence introducing an error in measurement of the volume.

Question.17. Why is it essential to remove the air bubbles from the jet of the burette before starting a titration?
Answer. Because the air bubbles may escape any time during the titration and thus affecting the volume of the titrant.

Question.18. What is the weight of the rider placed on 7 the division?
Answer. $0.0002 \times 7 = 0.0014$ g.

Where, n = no. of electrons gained or lost by 1 molecule during reduction or oxidation reaction it is undergoing.

Question.12. How can $\frac{M}{10}$ solution be diluted to get 500 ml of $\frac{M}{10}$ solution?
Answer. Use the formula $M_1V_1 = M_2V_2$

$$\frac{1}{10} \times V_1 = \frac{1}{50} \times 500$$
$$V_1 = 100\ ml$$

Take 100ml of $\frac{M}{10}$ solution in standard flask of 500ml capacity. Make up the volume by adding water.

Question.13. Why do burette and pipette should be rinsed with the solution for which they are to be

Question.19. Why are chemical substances not directly weighed in a chemical balance?
Answer. Because the chemicals may corrode the answer.

Question.20. What is the minimum weight that can be weighed by the chemical balance?
Answer. 2×10^{-4} g is the minimum weight that can be weighed on a usual chemical balance (using a rider).

Question.21. Which indicator is used in the titration of sodium carbonate against hydrochloric acid and what is the color change at the end point?
Answer. Methyl orange is used as an indicator. It changes its color from yellow to light pink at the end-point.

Question.22. Why is methyl orange not an Arrhenius base?
Answer. An Arrhenius base is one which produces hydroxide ions in aqueous solution. Methyl orange does not furnish OH^- ions in solution. Rather, it accepts proton, thus it is a Bronsted-Lowry base.

Question.23. What is the difference between an end point and an equivalence point?
Answer. In any titration, end point is the point where the indicator changes its color while the equivalence point is the point where the chemical reaction is completed stoichiometrically i.e., a stage at which equivalent amounts of acid reacts with equivalent

amounts of base. End point may or may not be equal to the equivalence point of the reaction.

Question.24. Can you directly prepare the standard solutions of HCl, HNO$_3$ and H$_2$SO$_4$?
Answer. No, the standard solutions of HCl, HNO, and H$_2$SO, cannot be prepared directly because all of these are used as secondary standard solutions.

Question.25. Can we titrate Na$_2$CO$_3$ solution against oxalic acid?
Answer. No, because no indicator gives a definite change in color at the end point.

Question.26. What is a titrant?
Answer. Titrant is the reagent of known concentration in titration, which is taken in the burette.

Question.27. What is a titrant?
Answer. It is the substance being titrated. It is taken in titration (or conical) flask.

Question.28. Define strength of a solution.
Answer. Strength of a solution is the amount of the solute present in a definite volume of the solution.

Question.29. How is an analytical balance different from a physical balance?
Answer. An analytical balance is more sensitive than physical balance and it can weigh up to 4 places of decimal.

Question.30. What is the maximum weight that can be weighed on a chemical balance?
Answer. Chemical or analytical balance can be used to weigh the mass of a substance maximum up to 100 grams.

Question.31. On what principle, is weighing by using rider based?
Answer. Principle of moment is applied for weighing of chemicals by using rider.

Question.32. Why are forceps always used for handling the weights?
Answer. Forceps are always used for handling the weights so that no impurity may stick to the weights and we can get more accurate results.

Question.33. Which weights are called fractional weights?

Answer. Milligram (mg) weights are called fractional weights.

Question.34. Define normality.
Answer. Normality of a solution is defined as the number of gram-equivalents of solute per liter of solution

Normality N = Number of gram - equivalents of solute
Volume of solution or Normality

$$= \frac{\text{Mass of solute (in grams) per liter of solution}}{\text{Gram - equivalent mass of the solute}}$$

Question.35. What do you mean by a molar solution?
Answer. A solution containing one gram mole of solute per liter of solution is called molar solution.

Question.36. Why are standard solutions always prepared in a volumetric flask?
Answer. Volumetric flask is always used to maintain precision while preparing or diluting the standard solution.

Question.37. What mass of oxalic acid is required to prepare 250 ml of 0.05 M oxalic acid solution?
Answer.

$$0.05\text{M} = \frac{\text{Mass of oxalic acid (in g)} \times 1000}{126 \times 250}$$
$$= 1.575\text{g of oxalic acid}$$

Hence, 1.575 g of oxalic acid is dissolved in 250 ml of distilled water to get 0.05 M or $\frac{M}{20}$ oxalic acid solution.

Question.38. Can solid NaOH be used to prepare its standard solution?
Answer. No, because it is deliquescent or hygroscopic in nature, i.e., it absorbs moisture from air.

Question.39. What type of substances can be used for preparing standard solution?
Answer. A substance fulfilling the following criteria can be used for preparing standard solutions:
(i) It should be easily available in pure and dry form.
(ii) It should not be hygroscopic, deliquescent or efflorescent in nature.
(iii) It should not be oxidised by air.
(iv) It should be readily soluble and its solution should be stable.

Question.40. What is the minimum weight that can be weighed by the chemical balance?

Answer. 2×10^{-4} g is the minimum weight that can be weighed by the chemical balance using a rider.

Question.41. Why should the last drop of the solution not be blown out of a pipette?
Answer. Because the drops left in the jet end is extra of the volume measured by pipette.

Question.42. Explain the term basicity of an acid and acidity of a base.
Answer. Number of replaceable hydroxyls (OH^-)ions furnished by a molecule of the base is known as its acidity and the number of replaceable hydrogens (H^+)ions furnished by a molecule of an acid is called basicity of an acid.

Question.43. What is meant by the term concordant readings?
Answer. The readings in volumetric analysis which differ by less than 0.05ml are called concordant readings.

Question.44. Can one take oxalic acid solution in the burette and sodium hydroxide solution in the titration flask? Point out the limitations of doing so, if any.
Answer. No, because if NaOH solution is taken in the conical or titration flask, the color change at the end point would be pink to colorless. The accuracy in noting this change may be less as compared to change from colorless to pink. Secondly, since NaOH is more corrosive in nature out of the two, therefore, taking it in the burette eliminates the chances of it going into the mouth while pipetting.

Question.45. What color change phenolphthalein shows when it is used as an indicator in acid-base titration?

Answer. Phenolphthalein turns from colorless (in acidic medium) to pink (in basic medium).

Question.46. How will you prepare 0.05M sodium carbonate solution?
Answer.

$$\text{Molarity} = \frac{W_{Na_2CO_3}}{\text{Molecular weight}} \times \frac{1000}{250}$$

$$0.05 = \frac{W_{Na_2CO_3}}{106} \times \frac{1000}{250}$$

$$W_{Na_2CO_3} = \frac{106}{20 \times 4} = 1.325g$$

$$\Rightarrow 0.05 = \frac{W_{Na_2CO_3}}{106} \times \frac{1000}{250}$$

$$\Rightarrow W_{Na_2CO_3} = \frac{106}{20 \times 4} = 1.325g$$

$\therefore$ 1.325g of Na_2CO_3 should be dissolved in 250 ml of distilled water to get 0.05 M solution.

Question.47. Though, sodium carbonate is a salt yet its aqueous solution is weakly alkaline in nature. Explain why?
Answer. Sodium carbonate is a salt of a strong base (NaOH) and a weak acid (H_2CO_3) and hence releases hydroxide ions in larger concentration than hydrogen ions. Hence, it is alkaline in aqueous solution.

Question.48. How can you determine the acidity of sodium carbonate solution?
Answer. Acidity of salt is equal to the total valency of metal ion. In sodium carbonate(Na_2CO_3), two sodium ions are present, therefore acidity of Na_2CO_3 equals to 2.

Question.49. What is the common name of sodium carbonate?
Answer. Washing soda

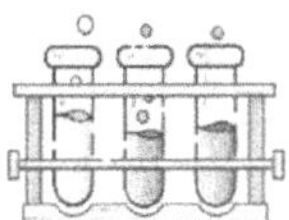

SYSTEMATIC QUALITATIVE ANALYSIS

AIM

Determination of one cation and one anion in a given salt

Cations. $Pb^{2+}, Cu^{2+}, Al^{3+}, Fe^{3+}, Mn^{2+}, Zn^{2+}, Co^{2+}, Ni^{2+}, Ca^{2+}, Sr^{2+}, Ba^{2+}, Mg^{2+}, NH_4^+$.

Anions. $CO_3^{2-}, S^{2-}, SO_3^{2-}, SO_4^{2-}, NO_2^-, NO_3^-, Cl^-, Br^-, I^-, PO_4^{3-}, C_2O_4^{2-}, CH_3COO^-$.

(Note. Insoluble salts excluded)

QUALITATIVE ANALYSIS

Analytical chemistry deals with qualitative and quantitative analysis of the substances. In inorganic qualitative analysis, the given compound is analyzed for the radicals, i.e., cation and the anion, that it contains. Physical procedures like noting the color, smell or taste of the substance have very limited scope because of the corrosive, poisonous nature of the chemical compounds. Therefore, what one has to resort to is the chemical analysis of the substance that has to be carried out along with the physical examination of the compound under consideration.

The common procedure for testing any unknown sample is to make its solution and then test this solution for the ions present in it. There are separate procedures for detecting cations and anions, therefore qualitative analysis is studied under cation analysis and anion analysis. The systematic procedure for qualitative analysis of an inorganic salt involves the following steps:

a) Preliminary tests

    I.   Physical appearance (color and smell).

    II.   Dry heating test.

    III.   Charcoal cavity test.

    IV.   Charcoal cavity and cobalt nitrate test.

    V.   Flame test.

    VI.   Borax bead test.

    VII.   Dilute acid test.

    VIII.   Potassium permanganate test.

    IX.   Concentrated sulfuric acid test.

    X.   Tests for sulphate, phosphate and borate.

b) Wet tests for acid radical.

c) Wet tests (group analysis) for basic radical. **Physical Examination of The Salt**

The physical examination of the unknown salt involves the study of color, smell and density. The test is not much reliable but is certainly helpful in identifying some colored cations. Characteristic smell helps to identify some ions such as ammonium, acetate and Sulfide.

Experiment	Observations	Inference
1. Color	Blue or Bluish green Light green Dark brown Green Pink Light pink, flesh color or earthy color White	Cu^{2+} Fe^{2+} Fe^{3+} Ni^{2+} Co^{2+} Mn^{2+} Shows the absence of Cu^{2+}, Fe^{2+}, Fe^{3+}, Ni^{2+}, Mn^{2+}, CO^{2+}
2. Smell Take a pinch of the salt between your fingers and rub with a drop of water	Ammoniacal smell Vinegar like smell Smell like that of rotten eggs	NH_4^+ CH_3COO^- S^{2-}
3. Density	(i) Heavy (ii) Light fluffy powder	Salt of Pb^{2+}, or Ba^{2+} Carbonate
4. Deliquescence	Salt absorbs moisture and becomes paste like	(i) If colored, may be $Cu(NO_3)_2$, $FeCl_3$. (ii) If colorless, may be $Zn(NO_3)_2$, chlorides of Zn^{2+}, Mg^{2+} etc.

Note:
1. *If you have touched any salt, wash your hands at onte. It may be corrosive to skin.*
2. *Never taste any salt, it may be poisonous. Salts of arsenic and mercury are highly poisonous.*
3. *Salts like sodium sulphide, sodium nitrite, potassium nitrite, develop a yellow colour.*

DRY HEATING TEST

This test is performed by heating a small amount of salt in a dry test tube. Quite valuable information can be gathered by carefully performing and noting the observations here. On heating some salts undergo decomposition thus evolving the gases or may undergo characteristic changes in the color of residue. These observations are tabulated below (Table 9.2) along with the inferences that you can draw.

Table 9.2. Dry Heating Test

Observations	Inference

1. **Gas evolved**
  (a) **Colorless and odourless gas**
      CO_2 gas turns lime water milky	

(b) **Colorless gas with odour** (i) H_2S gas—Smells like rotten eggs, turns lead acetate paper black.	S^{2-}
(ii) SO_2 gas—Smells like burning Sulphur, turns acidified potassium dichromate paper green.	$SO_3{}^{2-}$
(iii) HCl gas—Pungent smell, white fumes with ammonia, white ppt with silver nitrate solution.	Cl^-,
(iv) Acetic acid vapors—Characteristic vinegar like smell.	CH_3COO-
(v) NH_3 gas—Characteristic smell, turns Nessler's solution brown.	$NH_4{}^+$
(c) **Colored gases**—Pungent smell (i) NO_2 gas—Reddish brown, turns ferrous sulphate solution black.	NO_2^- or NO_3^-
(ii) Cl_2 gas—Greenish yellow, turns starch iodide paper blue.	Cl^-,
(iii) Br_2 vapors—Reddish brown, turns starch paper orange yellow.	$Br-$
(iv) I_2 vapors—Dark violet, turns starch paper blue.	$I-$

2. **Sublimate formed**
  (a) White sublimate
  (b) Black sublimate accompanied by violet vapors
	$NH_4{}^+$
	
	$I-$

3. **Decrepitation** The salt decrepitates.	A salt having no water of crystallisation. For example, $Pb(NO_3)_2$, NaCl, KBr.
4. **Swelling** The salt swells up into voluminous mass.	$PO_4{}^{3-}$ indicated

5. **Residue**
  (i) Yellow when hot white when cold
  (ii) Brown when hot and yellow when cold
  (iii) White salt becomes black on heating
  (iv) White residue, glows on heating
  (v) Original salt blue becomes white on heating
  (vi) Colored salt becomes brown or black on heating.
	Zn^{2+}
	Pb^{2+}
	CH_3COO- indicated
	Ba^{2+}, Sr^{2+}, Ca^{2+}, Mg^{2+}, etc.
	
	Hydrated $CuSO_4$ indicated

CHARCOAL CAVITY TEST

This test is based on the fact that metallic carbonates when heated in a charcoal cavity decompose to give corresponding oxides. The oxides appear as colored incrustation or residue in the cavity. In certain cases, the oxides formed partially undergo reduction to the metallic state producing metallic beads or scales. Examples:

a)
$$(ZnSO)_4 + Na_2CO_3 \longrightarrow ZnCO_3 + Na_2SO_4$$
$$ZnCO_3 \longrightarrow ZnO + CO_2 \uparrow$$

Yellow when hot,
white when cold

b)
$$Pb(NO_3)_2 + Na_2CO_3 \longrightarrow PbCO_3 + 2NaNO_3$$
$$PbCO_3 \longrightarrow PbO + CO_2 \uparrow$$
$$PbO + C \longrightarrow Pb + CO \uparrow$$

Bead

c)
$$CuSO_4 + Na_2CO_3 \longrightarrow CuCO_3 + Na_2SO_4$$
$$CuCO_3 \longrightarrow CuO + CO_2 \uparrow$$
$$CuO + C \longrightarrow Cu + CO \uparrow$$

Reddish
scales

PROCEDURE

While performing charcoal cavity test, make a small cavity on a charcoal block with the help of borer as shown in Fig. 9.2. Mix small amount of salt with double its quantity of sodium carbonate. Place it in the cavity made on the block of

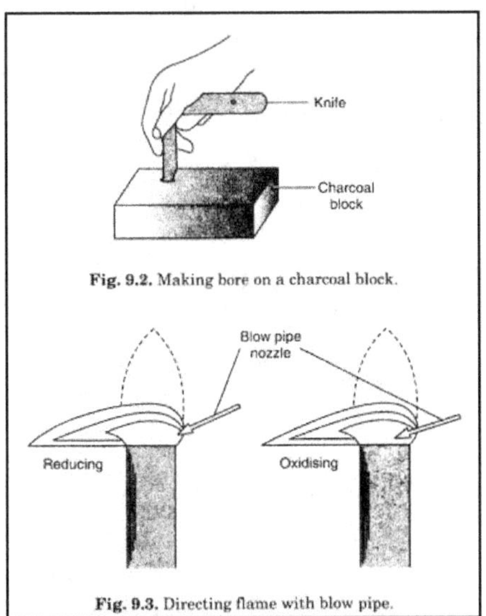

Fig. 9.2. Making bore on a charcoal block.

Fig. 9.3. Directing flame with blow pipe.

charcoal. Moisten with a drop of water and direct the reducing flame of the Bunsen Burner on the cavity by means of a mouth blowpipe as shown in Fig. 9.3. Heat strongly for some time and draw inference according to the Table.

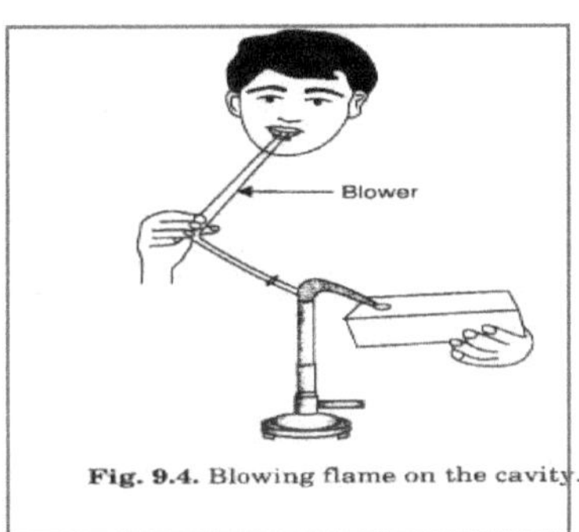

Fig. 9.4. Blowing flame on the cavity.

Observations			Inference
Incrustation or Residue		**Metallic bead**	
Hot	**Cold**		
Yellow	White	None	Zn^{2+}
Brown	Yellow	Grey bead which marks the paper	Pb^{2+}
None	None	Red beads or scales	Cu^{2+}
White residue which glows	None	None	Ba^{2+}, Ca^{2+}, Mg^{2+}
Black	None	None	Nothing definite— generally colored salt

To obtain a reducing flame with the help of a mouth blow pipe, make the Bunsen Burner flame luminous by closing the air holes of the Burner. Keep the nozzle of the blow pipe just outside the flame and blow gently on to the cavity.

COBALT NITRATE TEST

This test is applied to those salts which leave white residue in charcoal cavity test.

The test is based on the fact that cobalt nitrate decomposes on heating to give cobalt oxide, CoO. This combines with the metallic oxides, present as white residue in the charcoal cavity forming colored compounds. For example, when a magnesium salt undergoes charcoal cavity test, a white residue of MgO is left behind. This on treatment with cobalt nitrate and subsequent heating forms a double salt of the formula MgO-CoO which is pink in color. In addition to metallic oxides, phosphates and borates also react with cobalt oxide to form $Co_3(PO_4)_2$ and $Co_3(BO_3)_2$ which are blue in color.

Some of the reactions involved are given below:

   i. Zinc salt:

$$2Co(NO_3)_2 \xrightarrow{\Delta} 2CoO + 4NO_2 + O_2 \quad ZnO + CoO \longrightarrow ZnO \cdot CoO \text{ (Green)}$$

   ii. Magnesium salt:

$$MgO + CoO \longrightarrow MgO.CoO \text{ (Pink)}$$

PROCEDURE

Put one or two drops of cobalt nitrate solution on the white residue left after charcoal cavity test. Heat for one or two minutes by means of a blow pipe in oxidising flame. Observe the color of the residue and draw inferences from Table

Cobalt Nitrate-Charcoal Cavity Test

Color of the Residue	Inference
Green	Zn^{2+}
Pink	Mg^{2+}
Blue	PO_4^{3-}
Black	It is due to the formation of CoO. No definite indication.

BORAX BEAD TEST

Certain salts on reacting with cone. HCl from their chlorides, that are volatile in non-luminous flame. Their vapors impart characteristic color to the flame. This color can give reliable information of the presence of certain basic radicals.

For proceeding to this test, the paste of the mixture with cone. HCl is introduced into the flame with the help of platinum wire (Fig. 9.5).

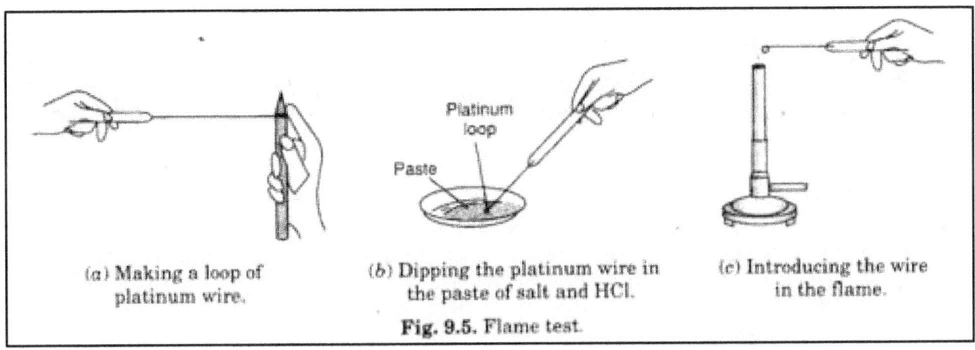

Fig. 9.5. Flame test.

PROCEDURE

Clean the platinum wire by dipping it in some cone. HCl taken on a watch glass and then heating strongly in the flame. This process is repeated till the wire imparts no color to the flame. Now prepare a paste of the mixture with cone. HCl on a clean watch glass. Place small amount of this paste on platinum wire loop and introduce it into the flame. Note the color imparted to the flame with naked eye and through blue glass.

Color of the Flame		Inference
With naked eye	**Through blue glass**	
1. Brick-red (not persistent)	Light yellowish green	Ca^{2+}
2. Crimson red (persistent)	Crimson	Sr^{2+}
3. Persistent grassy-green (appears after prolonged heating)	Green	Ba^{2+}
4. Bright-bluish green	Visible	Cu^{2+}
5. Green flashes		Zn^{2+} and Mn^{2+} salts
6. Dull bluish white	White	Pb^{2+}

BORAX BEAD TEST

This test is performed only for colored salts.

Borax, $Na_2B_4O_7.10H_2O$, on heating gets fused and loses water of crystallisation. It swells up into a fluffy white porous mass which then melts into a colorless liquid which later forms, a clear transparent glassy bead consisting of boric anhydride and sodium metaborate.

$$Na_2B_4O_7 \cdot 10H_2O \rightarrow Na_2B_4O_7 + 10H_2O \uparrow \quad Na_2B_4O_7 \rightarrow \underset{\text{Boric anhydride}}{B_2O_3} + \underset{\text{Sodium metaborate}}{2NaBO_2}$$

Boric anhydride is non-volatile. When it is reacted with colored metallic salt, a characteristic-colored bead of metal metaborate is formed.

$$Cr_2(SO_4)_3 + 3B_2O_3 \rightarrow \underset{\text{Deep Green}}{2Cr(BO_2)_3} + 3SO_3$$

In the cases where different colored beads are obtained in the oxidising and reducing flames, metaborates in various oxidation states of metals are formed. For example, in oxidising flame, copper forms blue copper metaborate.

$$Na_2B_4O_7 + CuSO_4 \rightarrow 2NaBO_2 + \underset{\text{Blue}}{Cu(BO_2)_2} + SO_3$$

In reducing flame cupric metaborate is reduced to metallic copper, which is red and opaque.

$$2Cu(BO_2)_2 + 4NaBO_2 + 2C \rightarrow \underset{\text{Red opaque}}{2Cu} + 2Na_2B_4O_7 + 2CO$$

PROCEDURE

Borax, $Na_2B_4O_7.10H_2O$ is heated in the loop of platinum wire, it swells and forms transparent colorless glassy bead. When this hot bead is touched with small amount of colored salt and is heated again, it acquires a characteristic color. The color of bead gives indication of the type of the cation present. The color of the bead is noted separately in oxidising and in reducing flame (Fig. 12.6).

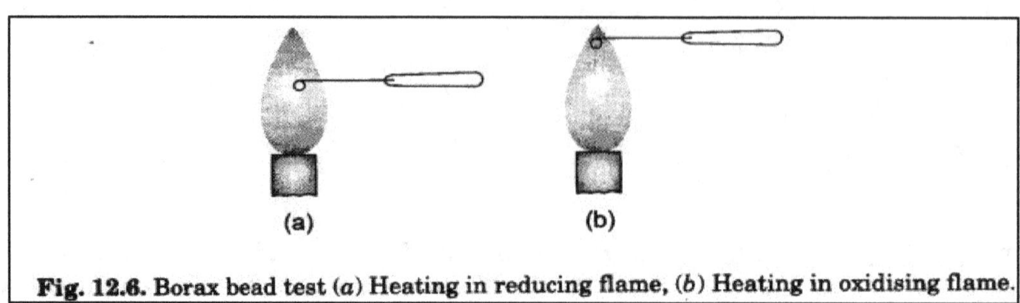

Fig. 12.6. Borax bead test (*a*) Heating in reducing flame, (*b*) Heating in oxidising flame.

Color of the bead		Inference
In Oxidising flame	**In Reducing flame**	
1. Green when hot, light blue when cold.	Colorless when hot, opaque red when cold.	Cu^{2+}
2. Yellowish brown when hot, pale yellow when cold	Green, hot and cold.	Fe^{2+} or Fe^{3+}
3. Amethyst (pinkish violet) in both hot and cold.	Colorless, hot and cold.	Mn^{2+}
4. Brown when hot, pale brown when cold.	Grey or black when hot and opaque when cold	Ni^{2+}
5. Deep blue in both hot and cold	Deep blue in both hot and cold	Co^{2+}

To remove the head from platinum wire, heat the head to redness. Tap the rod with finger stroke, till the bead jumps off (Fig. 12.7).

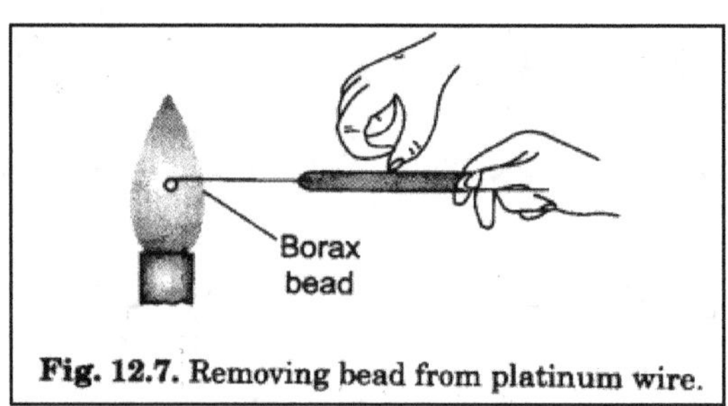

Fig. 12.7. Removing bead from platinum wire.

The identification of the acid radicals is first done on the basis of preliminary tests. Dry heating test is one of the preliminary tests performed earlier which may give some important information about the acid radical present. The other preliminary tests are based upon the fact that:

1. $CO_3^{\,2-}, S^{2-}, NO_2^{\,-}$ and $SO_3^{\,2-}$ react with dil. H_2SO_4 to give out CO_2, H_2S, NO_2 and SO_2 gases respectively which can be identified by certain tests.

2. $Cl^-, Br, I^-, NO_3^-, C_2O_4^{2-}$ and CH_3COO^- react with conc. H_2SO_4 but not with dil. H_2SO_4 to produce characteristic gases.

3. SO_4^{2-} and $PO_4{}^{3-}$ react neither with dil. H_2SO_4 nor with conc. H_2SO_4. These are therefore, identified by individual tests.

Thus, the acid radicals may be identified by performing the following tests in the order given below:

1. Dil. H_2SO_4 test. Treat a pinch of the salt with dil. H_2SO_4 and identify the gas evolved.
2. Conc. $H_{20}SO_4$ test. If no action takes place with dil. H_2SO_4, warm a pinch of the salt with conc. H_2SO_4 and identify the gas evolved.
3. Independent Group. ($SO_4{}^2$ and $PO_4{}^{3-}$). If the salt does not react with dil. H_2SO_4 as well as with conc. H_2SO_4, test for SO_4^{2-} and PO_4^{3-} by performing their individual tests.

Let us now discuss these tests in detail one by one.

Take a small quantity of the salt in a test-tube and add 1-2 ml of dilute sulfuric add. Identify the gas and draw.

Table 12.7. Dilute Sulfuric Acid Test

Observations	Inference	
	Gas	**Radical**
1. Colorless, odourless gas with brisk effervescence, turns lime water milky.	CO_2	CO_3^{2-}
2. Colorless gas, pungent smell, turns acidified potassium dichromate paper or solution green. Colorless gas with smell like that of rotten eggs, turns lead acetate paper black.	SO_2 H_2S	SO_3^{2-} S^{2-}
3. Reddish brown gas, pungent smell, turns ferrous sulphate solution black.	NO_2	NO_2^-
4. No gas is evolved.	$SO_3^2 - S^{2-}$	CO_3^{2-}

CHEMICAL REACTIONS INVOLVED IN DIL. H₂SO₄ TEST

Dilute H_2SO_4 (or dilute HCl) decomposes carbonates, sulphides and nitrites in cold to give gases. These gases on identification indicate the nature of the add radical present in the salt.

1. **Carbonates:** On treating the solid carbonate, CO_2 is given off in the cold with brisk effervescence.

$$CaCO_3 + H_2SO_4 \longrightarrow CaSO_4 + H_2O + CO_2 \uparrow$$

2. **Sulphides:** when treated with dil. H_2SO_4 give H_2S gas.

$$ZnS + H_2SO_4 \rightarrow ZnSO_4 + H_2S \uparrow$$

3. **Sulphites**: On treating solid sulphite with dil. H_2SO_4, SO_2 gas is evolved

$$ZnS + H_2SO_4 \rightarrow ZnSO_4 + H_2S \uparrow$$

Nitrites. On treating the solid nitrite with dil. H_2SO_4 nitric oxide (NO) gas is evolved which readily gives dense brown fumes of NO_2 with oxygen of the air.

$$
\begin{aligned}
KNO_2 + H_2SO_4 &\rightarrow [KHSO_4 + HNO_2] \times 3 \\
3HNO_2 &\rightarrow HNO_3 + H_2O + 2NO \\
3KNO_2 + 3H_2SO_4 &\rightarrow 3KHSO_4 + HNO_3 + H_2O + 2NO \\
2NO + O_2 &\rightarrow 2NO_2 \\
&\quad\; \text{Colorless} \quad \text{Brown} \\
&\qquad\qquad\qquad \text{fumes}
\end{aligned}
$$

POTASSIUM PERMANGANATE TEST

To a pinch of salt in test tube add about 2 ml of dilute sulfuric acid. Boil off any gas evolved, add little more of dilute acid and then potassium permanganate solution dropwise. Note the changes as given in Table 12.8. This test helps in detection of Cl^-, Br^-, I^-, $C_2O_4^{2-}$ and Fe^{2+} radicals.

Table 12.8. Potassium Permanganate Test

Observations	Inference
1. Potassium permanganate decolorised without the evolution of any gas.	Presence of Fe^{2+} salts.
2. Potassium permanganate decolorised:	
a. In cold	
i. With the evolution of chlorine.	Cl^-
ii. With the evolution of bromine.	Br^-
iii. With the evolution of iodine.	I^-
b. On warming on warming With evolution of CO_2	$C_2O_4^{2-}$
3. $KMnO_4$ not decolorised.	Absence of $Cl^-, Br^-, I^-, C_2O_4^{2-}$ and Fe^{2+}

Note:
1. *As sulphides are oxidised by KMnO₄ so they have to be completely decomposed by heating with dilute sulphuric acid before this test is performed.*
2. *Potassium permanganate oxidises Fe²⁺ salts in cold. Oil H₂SO₄ acid is added to the salt and heated till sulphides, sulphites and nitrites are completely decomposed. Then KMnO₄ is added dropwise to cold solution.*

CHEMICAL REACTIONS INVOLVED

$$2KMnO_4 + 3H_2SO_4 \longrightarrow K_2SO_4 + 2MnSO_4 + 3H_2O + 5[O]$$

1. Ferrous salts: $\quad 2FeSO_4 + H_2SO_4 + [O] \longrightarrow Fe_2(SO_4)_3 + H_2O$

2. Chlorides:

$$NaCl + H_2SO_4 \longrightarrow NaHSO_4 + HCl$$
$$2HCl + [O] \longrightarrow H_2O + Cl_2 \uparrow$$

3. Bromides:

$$NaBr + H_2SO_4 \longrightarrow NaHSO_4 + HBr$$
$$2HBr + [O] \longrightarrow H_2O + Br_2 \uparrow$$

4. Iodides:

$$NaI + H_2SO_4 \longrightarrow NaHSO_4 + HI$$
$$2HI + [O] \longrightarrow H_2O + I_2 \uparrow$$

5. Oxalates:

$$\underset{COONa}{COONa} + H_2SO_4 \longrightarrow \underset{COOH}{COOH} + Na_2SO_4$$

$$\underset{COOH}{COOH} + [O] \longrightarrow 2CO_2 \uparrow + H_2O$$

CONCENTRATED SULFURIC ACID TEST

This test is performed by treating small quantity of salt with cone, sulfuric acid (2-3 ml) in a test tube. Identify the gas evolved in cold and then on heating. Draw inferences from Table 12.9.

Table 12.9. Conc. Sulfuric Acid Test

Observations	Inference	
	Gas	Radical
1. Colorless gas with pungent smell, white fumes with aqueous ammonia, white ppt. with solution.	HCl	Cl^-
2. Reddish brown vapors with pungent smell, turns starch paper yellow. It does not turn solution black.	Br_2	Br^-
3. Deep violet vapors with pungent smell, turns starch paper blue. A sublimate is formed on the sides of the tube.	I_2 vapors	I^-
4. Reddish brown gas with pungent smell, turns solution black.	NO_2	NO_3^-
5. Colorless vapors, vinegar smell, turns blue litmus red.	CH_3COOH vapors	CH_3COO^-
6. A colorless gas with turns lime water milky and also a gas which burns with pale-bluish flame	$CO_2 + CO$	$C_2O_4^{2-}$
7. No gas/vapors evolved.	-	$Cl^-, Br^-, I^-, NO_3^-,$ CH_3COO^- absent

CHEMICAL REACTIONS INVOLVED IN CONC. H_2SO_4 TEST

1. Chlorides $\quad$ $NaCl + H_2SO_4 \longrightarrow \underset{\text{Sod. bisulphate}}{NaHSO_4} + HCl$

2. 2. Bromides $\quad$ $NaBr + H_2SO_4 \longrightarrow NaHSO_4 + HBr$

    $H_2SO_4 + 2HBr \longrightarrow SO_2 + Br_2 + 2H_2O$

3. Iodides $\quad$ $KI + H_2SO_4 \longrightarrow KHSO_4 + HI$

    $H_2SO_4 + 2HBr \longrightarrow SO_2 + Br_2 + 2I_2$

4. Nitrates $\quad$ $KNO_3 + H_2SO_4 \longrightarrow KHSO_4 + HNO_3$

    $4HNO_3 + \underset{\substack{\text{(Paper} \\ \text{pellet)}}}{C} \longrightarrow 4NO_2 \uparrow + CO_2 + 2H_2O$

5. Acetates $\quad$ $CH_3COONa + H_2SO_4 \longrightarrow NaHSO_4 + \underset{\text{Acetic acid}}{CH_3COOH}$

6. Oxalates $\quad$ $\begin{array}{c} COONa \\ | \\ COONa \end{array} + H_2SO_4 \longrightarrow Na_2SO_4 + CO_2 \uparrow + CO \uparrow + H_2O$

TESTS FOR INDEPENDENT RADICALS (SO_4^{2-} AND PO_4^{3-})

As already discussed, these radicals are not detected by dilute or concentrated H_2SO_4. They are tested individually.

1. SULPHATE (SO_4^{2-})

Boil a small amount of salt with dilute HCl in a test tube. Filter the contents, and to the filtrate add few drops of $BaCl_2$ solution. A white ppt. insoluble in conc. HCl indicates presence of sulphate.

2. PHOSPHATE (PO_4^{3-})

Add conc.HNO_3 to the salt in a test tube. Boil the contents and add excess of ammonium molybdate solution. A yellow precipitate indicates presence of phosphate.

CONFIRMATION OF ACID RADICALS BY WET TESTS

The acid radical indicated by dil. H_2SO_4 or conc. H_2SO_4 tests is further confirmed by wet tests.

Preparation of solution for wet tests of acid radicals

The confirmatory tests for acid radicals are performed with salt solutions. The solution used for the purpose is any one of the following:

1. Aqueous solution or 'water extract: Shake a little of the salt with water. If the salt dissolves, this aqueous solution obtained is used for the wet tests of acid radical and is called 'water extract' or 'W.E.'. If the salt is not completely soluble in water, the salt is shaken with water and is filtered. The filtrate is treated as water extract.

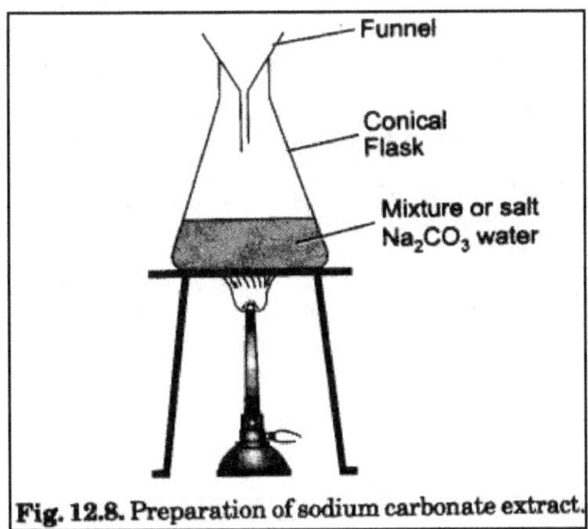

Fig. 12.8. Preparation of sodium carbonate extract.

2. Sodium carbonate extract: This is prepared only if the salt is insoluble in water. Preparation of Sodium Carbonate Extract. Mix about 1 g of the salt with about 2 g of pure sodium carbonate and boil it for 10-15 minutes with 20-25 ml of distilled water in a small conical flask having a funnel in its mouth (Fig. 12.8). The funnel acts as a condenser. This arrangement prevents the loss of water due to evaporation. Filter the solution, cool it and label it as sodium carbonate extract or S.E.

    Alternatively, sodium carbonate extract can be prepared in a test tube. A pinch of salt is mixed with double the amount of sodium carbonate and is boiled with distilled water for some time. The suspension obtained is filtered. The filtrate is sodium carbonate extract. (pg. 12 8). Preparation of sodium carbonate extract.

THEORY OF PREPARATION OF SODIUM CARBONATE EXTRACT

When the salts are boiled with strong solution of sodium carbonate, double decompo-sition takes place resulting in the formation of the carbonates of heavy metallic radicals and sodium salts of the acid radicals. The sodium salts of corresponding add radicals being soluble in water pass into the solution and carbonates of heavy metals are predicated.

$$ZnS(s) + Na_2CO_3(aq) \rightarrow ZnCO_3(s) \downarrow + Na_2S(aq)$$

HOW TO USE SODIUM CARBONATE EXTRACT

Sodium carbonate extract always contains unreacted sodium carbonate in solution which has to be destroyed before using the extract for various tests. To do this, the extract is acidified with some suitable acid and is boiled to expel carbon dioxide. The selection of add used for destroying excess Na$_2$CO$_3$ depends upon the radical to be identified.

Now we describe in detail the confirmatory tests for various add radicals discussed so far.

Confirmation of Carbonate, CO$_3^{2-}$

(Indicated in dilute acid test by occurrence of brisk effervescence and evolution of carbon dioxide).

Confirmation of soluble carbonate	Confirmation of insoluble carbonate
If the salt dissolves, soluble carbonate is indicated. 1. Dil. HCl test To one portion of the solution, add dil. HCl. Brisk effervescence and evolution of carbon dioxide which turns lime water milky confirms the presence of soluble carbonate. 2. Magnesium sulphate test To another portion of the solution, add magnesium sulphate solution. Formation of white precipitate in the cold confirms the presence of soluble carbonate.	If the salt remains insoluble, the presence of insoluble carbonate is indicated. To the salt add dil. HCl. Brisk effervescence and evolution of carbon dioxide which turns lime water milky confirms the presence of insoluble carbonate.

CONFIRMATION OF SULPHIDE, S^{2-}

(Indicated in dilute acid test by the evolution of hydrogen sulphide).

Experiment	Observations
1. Barium chloride test Take a portion of aqueous solution (or sodium carbonate extract and dil. acetic acid and boil off CO_2). Add barium chloride solution to it. Filter. To a portion of the above ppt. add dil. HCl.	A white ppt. is formed.
2. $KMnO_4$ test To a second part of the ppt. from (1) add a few drops of acidified potassium permanganate solution.	The ppt. dissolves with the evolution of sulphur dioxide. The pink color is discharged.
3. $K_2Cr_2O_7$ test To a portion of aqueous solution or sodium carbonate extract add potassium dichromate solution acidified with dil. H_2SO_4.	A green color is obtained.

Note:
1. *Do not use sodium carbonate extract for performing the tests of carbonates because it contains sodium carbonate.*
2. *Perform magnesium sulphate test only in case of soluble carbonates.*

CONFIRMATION OF SULPHIDE, S^{2-}

(Indicated in dilute acid test by the evolution of hydrogen sulphide).

Experiment	Observations
1. Sodium nitroprusside test Take a portion of aqueous solution (or sodium carbonate extract) in a test tube and add a few drops of sodium nitroprusside solution.	Purple or violet coloration is obtained.
2. Lead acetate test To a portion of aqueous solution (or sodium carbonate extract acidified with dil. acetic acid) add lead acetate solution.	A black ppt. is obtained.
3. Cadmium carbonate test To a portion of aqueous solution (or sodium carbonate extract) add a suspension of cadmium carbonate in water.	A yellow ppt. is formed.

CONFIRMATION OF NITRITE, NO_2^-

(Indicated in dilute acid test by the evolution of brown vapors of nitrogen peroxide)

Experiment	Observations
1. Ferrous sulphate test To a portion of aqueous solution, add some dil. acetic acid and ferrous sulphate solution.	A dark brown or black coloration is obtained.
2. Starch-iodide test To a portion of aqueous solution add a few drops of dil. H_2SO_4 and a few drops of potassium iodide solution followed by freshly prepared starch solution.	A blue solution is obtained.
3. Diphenylamine test To a portion of aqueous solution, add a few drops of diphenylamine.	A deep blue coloration is obtained.

CHEMICAL REACTION

Ions Involved in the Confirmation of Carbonate, Sulphide and Nitrite Carbonate (CO_3^{2-})

1. **Reaction with dil. HCl**

   Carbonates on reaction with dil. HCl give CO_2 gas which turns lime water milky. In case of soluble carbonates this test is performed with water extract and in case of insoluble carbonates this test is performed with the solid salt.

$$CaCO_3 + 2HCl \longrightarrow CaCl_2 + CO_2 + H_2O$$

$$\underset{\text{Lime water}}{Ca(OH)_2} + CO_2 \longrightarrow \underset{\text{Milkiness}}{CaCO_3} + H_2O$$

2. **Magnesium sulphate test**

This test is-performed in case of soluble carbonates only

$$Na_2CO_3 + MgSO_4 \rightarrow MgCO_3 \downarrow + Na_2SO_4$$
$$\text{(White ppt.)}$$

SULPHITE (SO_3^{2-})

1. **Barium chloride test**

$$Na_2SO_3 + BaCl_2 \rightarrow 2NaCl + BaSO_3 \downarrow$$
$$\text{(White ppt.)}$$
$$BaSO_3 + 2HCl \rightarrow BaCl_2 + SO_2 \uparrow + H_2O$$

2. **Potassium permanganate test**

$$2KMnO_4 + 3H_2SO_4 \rightarrow K_2SO_4 + 2MnSO_4 + 3H_2O + 5[O]$$
$$Na_2SO_3 + [O] \rightarrow Na_2SO_4$$

3. **Potassium dichromate test**

$$K_2Cr_2O_7 + 4H_2S O_4 \rightarrow K_2SO_4 + Cr_2(SO_4)_3 + 4H_2O + 3[O]$$
$$\text{(orange)} \qquad \text{(green)}$$
$$Na_2SO_3 + [O] \rightarrow Na_2SO_4$$

SULPHIDE (S^{2-})

1. **Sod. nitroprusside test**

$$Na_2S + Na_2[Fe(CN)_5NO] \rightarrow Na_4[Fe(CN)_5NOS]$$
$$\text{Sod. nitroprusside} \qquad \text{(Violet or Purple color)}$$

2. **Lead acetate test**

$$Na_2S + (CH_3COO)_2Pb \rightarrow PbS \downarrow + 2CH_3COONa$$
$$\text{Blackppt.}$$

3. **Cadmium carbonate test**

$$Na_2S + CdCO_3 \rightarrow CdS \downarrow + Na_2CO_3$$
$$\text{Yellow ppt.}$$

NITRITE (NO^{2-})

1. **Ferrous sulphate test**

$$KNO_2 + CH_3COOH \rightarrow CH_3COOK + HNO_2$$
$$3HNO_2 \rightarrow HNO_3 + 2NO + H_2O$$
$$FeSO_4 + NO \rightarrow FeSO_4 \cdot NO$$
$$\text{(Dark brown)}$$

2. **Potassium iodide test**

$$2KI + 2H_2SO_4 + 2HNO_2 \rightarrow 2KHSO_4 + I_2 + 2NO + 2H_2O$$

I_2 turns starch paper blue.

CONFIRMATION OF CHLORIDE, Cl⁻

(No action with dilute H_2SO_4 but decomposed by conc. H_2SO_4 with the evolution of HCl gas).

Experiment	Observations
1. Silver nitrate test Acidify a portion of aqueous solution (or sodium carbonate extract) with dil. HNO_3. Boil for some time, cool and add $AgNO_3$ solution.	A white ppt. is formed which is soluble in ammonium hydroxide.
2. Manganese dioxide test Heat a pinch of the salt with a small quantity of MnO_2 and conc. H_2SO_4.	Evolution of greenish yellow gas having a pungent irritating smell. It turns moist starch-iodide paper blue.
3. Chromyl chloride test Mix a small quantity of the salt with a small amount of powdered potassium dichromate. Take the mixture in a test tube and add conc. H_2SO_4. Heat the tube and pass the red vapors evolved into the gas detector containing NaOH solution. To the yellow solution thus obtained, add dil. CH_3COOH and lead acetate solution.	A yellow ppt. is formed.

CONFIRMATION OF BROMIDE, Br⁻

(No action with dilute H_2SO_4 but decomposed by conc. H_2SO_4 with the evolution of bromine vapors).

Experiment	Observations
1. Silver nitrate test Acidify a portion of aqueous solution (or sodium carbonate extract) with dil. HNO_3. Boil, cool and add $AgNO_3$ solution.	A light-yellow ppt. is obtained which is partially soluble in NH_4OH.
2. Manganese dioxide test Heat a small quantity of the salt with solid MnO_2 and conc. H_2SO_4.	Evolution of yellowish-brown vapors of bromine which turn starch paper yellow.
3. Chlorine water test Acidify a portion of aqueous solution (or sodium carbonate extract) with dil. HCl and add 1-2 ml of carbon disulphide and then chlorine water. Shake vigorously and allow to stand.	Carbon di-sulphide layer acquires orange coloration.

Note:
Chlorine water is prepared by adding dropwise conc. HCl to a small volume of KMnO₄ solution till the pink colour is just discharged, the resulting solution is chlorine water.

CONFIRMATION OF IODIDE, I

(No action with dilute H_2SO_4 but decomposed by cone. H_2SO_4 with the evolution of vapors of iodine).

Experiment	Observations
1. Silver nitrate test Acidify a portion of aqueous solution (or sodium carbonate extract) with dil. HNO_3. Boil, cool and add $AgNO_3$ solution.	A yellow ppt. is formed which is insoluble in NH_4OH.
2. Manganese dioxide test Heat a small quantity of the salt with a little MnO_2 and conc. H_2SO_4.	Evolution of violet vapors of iodine which turn starch paper blue.
3. Chlorine water test Acidify a part of the aqueous solution (or sodium carbonate extract) with dil. HCl, add 1-2 ml of carbon di-sulphide and then chlorine water. Shake vigorously and allow to stand.	Carbon di-sulphide layer acquires a violet coloration.

CONFIRMATION OF NITRATE, NO^{3-}

(No action with dilute acids but decomposed by cone. H_2SO_4 with the evolution of brown vapors of nitrogen peroxide).

Experiment	Observations
1. Diphenylamine test Add a few drops of diphenylamine to a part of aqueous solution of the salt.	A deep blue coloration is obtained.
2. Copper chips test Heat a small quantity of the original salt with concentrated sulfuric acid and a few copper chips.	Dark brown fumes of nitrogen dioxide are evolved.
3. Ring Test Add a small quantity of freshly prepared solution of ferrous sulphate to a part of the aqueous solution and then pour concentrated sulfuric acid slowly along the sides of the test tube as shown in (Fig. 12.9).	A dark brown ring is formed at the junction of the layers of the acid and the solution.

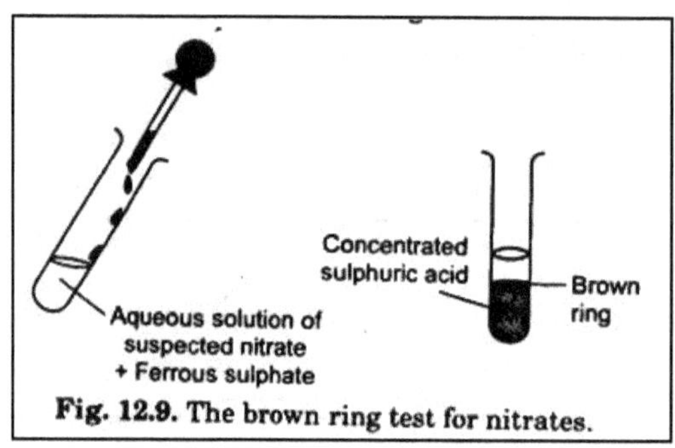

Fig. 12.9. The brown ring test for nitrates.

CONFIRMATION OF ACETATE, CH₃COO⁻

(No action with dilute acids but decomposed by cone. H_2SO_4 with the evolution of CH_3COOH vapors

Experiment	Observations
1. Oxalic acid test Take a small quantity of the salt on a watch glass. Mix it with solid oxalic acid. Prepare paste of it with a few drops of water. Rub the paste and smell.	Smell like that of vinegar.
2. Ester test Take a small quantity of the salt in a test-tube. Add conc. H_2SO_4 (2ml) and heat. Now add ethyl alcohol (1 ml). Shake. Pour the contents of the tube in a beaker full of water. Stir.	Pleasant fruity smell of ester.

3. Ferric chloride test
Take water extract of the salt. Add neutral ferric chloride solution. Filter. Divide the filtrate into two portions.
  i. To one part, add dil. HCl.
  ii. To second part, add water and boil.
	Reddish colored filtrate.
	
	Reddish color disappears.
	
	Reddish brown ppt.

CONFIRMATION OF OXALATE, C₂O₄⁻

(No action with dilute acids but decomposed by cone. H_2SO_4 with the evolution of CO_2 and CO gas)

Experiment	Observations
1. Calcium chloride test Take water extract (or soda extract if salt is insoluble in water). Add small amount dil acetic acid and boil off CO_2. Add calcium chloride solution. Add dil HNO_3 to the white ppt and warm.	A white ppt. is formed. The ppt. dissolves.
2. Potassium permanganate test Take a pinch of the salt in test tube and add dil. sulfuric acid. Warm to $60 - 70°C$ and add $2 - 3$ drops of $KMnO_4$ solution.	The pink color of $KMnO_4$ solution is decolorized with the evolution of CO_2 gas.

Chemical Reactions Involved in the Confirmation of Chloride, Bromide, Iodide, Nitrate Acetate and Oxalate.

CHLORIDE (Cl⁻)

1. Silver nitrate test

$$NaCl + AgNO_3 \longrightarrow \underset{\text{White ppt.}}{AgCl \downarrow} + NaNO_3$$

$$AgCl + 2NH_4OH \longrightarrow \underset{\text{Soluble complex}}{[Ag(NH_3)_2]Cl} + 2H_2O$$

2. MnO₂ test

$$2NaCl + MnO_2 + 3H_2SO_4 \longrightarrow 2NaHSO_4 + MnSO_4 + 2H_2O + Cl_2 \uparrow$$

3. Chromyl chloride test

$$4NaCl + K_2Cr_2O_7 + 3H_2SO_4 \longrightarrow 2Na_2SO_4 + K_2SO_4 + \underset{\text{Chromyl chloride}}{2CrO_2Cl_2} + 3H_2O$$

$$CrO_2Cl_2 + 4NaOH \longrightarrow \underset{\text{Sod. chromate}}{Na_2CrO_4} + 2H_2O + 2NaCl$$

$$Na_2CrO_4 + (CH_3COO)_2Pb \longrightarrow \underset{\substack{\text{Lead chromate} \\ \text{(Yellow ppt.)}}}{PbCrO_4} \downarrow + 2CH_3COONa$$

BROMIDE (Br$^-$)

1. Silver nitrate test

$$KBr + AgNO_3 \longrightarrow KNO_3 + \underset{\text{(Pale yellow ppt.)}}{AgBr} \downarrow$$

Pale yellow ppt. of silver bromide are sparingly soluble in ammonium hydroxide.

2. MnO$_2$ test

$$2KBr + MnO_2 + 3H_2SO_4 \longrightarrow 2KHSO_4 + MnSO_4 + 2H_2O + Br_2$$

3. Chlorine water test

$$2KBr + Cl_2 \longrightarrow 2KCl + Br_2$$

Bromine being soluble in CCl_4 imparts an orange color to the CCl_4 layer.

IODIDE (I$^-$)

1. Silver nitrate test

$$KI + AgNO_3 \longrightarrow KNO_3 + \underset{\text{(yellow ppt.)}}{AgI}$$

2. MnO$_2$ test

$$2KI + MnO_2 + 3H_2SO_4 \longrightarrow 2KHSO_4 + MnSO_4 + 2H_2O + I_2$$

3. Chlorine water test

$$2KI + Cl_2 \longrightarrow 2KCl + I_2$$

Iodine being soluble in CCl_4 imparts a violet color to the CCl_4 layer.

Nitrate (NO$_3^-$)

1. Copper test

$$2KNO_3 + H_2SO_4 \longrightarrow K_2SO_4 + 2HNO_3$$

$$4HNO_3 + Cu \longrightarrow Cu(NO_3)_2 + \underset{\text{(Reddish brown)}}{2NO_2} + 2H_2O$$

2. Ring Test

$$KNO_3 + H_2SO_4 \longrightarrow KHSO_4 + HNO_3$$
$$6FeSO_4 + 3H_2SO_4 + 2HNO_3 \longrightarrow 3Fe_2(SO_4)_3 + 4H_2O + 2NO$$
$$FeSO_4 + NO + 5H_2O \longrightarrow [Fe(NO)(H_2O)_5]SO_4$$

(Brown ring)

ACETATE (CH_3COO^-)

1. Oxalic acid test

$$\begin{matrix} COOH \\ | \\ COOH \end{matrix} + 2CH_3COONa \longrightarrow \begin{matrix} COOHNa \\ | \\ COONa \end{matrix} + 2CH_3COOH$$

Acetic acid (Vinegar smell)

2. Ester test

$$2CH_3COONa + H_2SO_4 \longrightarrow Na_2SO_4 + 2CH_3COOH$$
$$CH_3COOH + C_2H_5OH \longrightarrow CH_3COOC_2H_5 + H_2O$$

Ethyl acetate

(Fruity smell)

3. Ferric chloride test

$$3CH_3COONa + FeCl_3 \longrightarrow (CH_3COO)_3Fe + 3NaCl$$
$$(CH_3COO)_3Fe + 2H_2O \longrightarrow (CH_3COO)(OH)_2Fe \downarrow + 2CH_3COOH$$

Reddish brown ppt.

ORALATE ($C_8O_4^{2-}$)

1. Calcium chloride test

$$(NH_4)_2C_2O_4 + CaCl_2 \longrightarrow CaC_2O_4 \downarrow + 2NH_4Cl$$

White ppt.

2. Potassium permanganate test

$$2KMnO_4 + 3H_2SO_4 + 5\begin{matrix}COOH \\ | \\ COOH\end{matrix} \longrightarrow K_2SO_4 + 2MnSO_4 + 10CO_2 \uparrow + 8H_2O$$

CONFIRMATION OF SULPHATE, SO_4^{2-}

(Not indicated in dilute and concentrated H_2SO_4 acid tests).

Experiment	Observations
1. Barium chloride test To a part of the aqueous solution of the salt add barium chloride solution.	A white ppt. is formed which is insoluble in dil HCl.
2. Match stick test Mix a small amount of the salt with sodium carbonate and a little powdered charcoal so as to get a paste. Take some of this paste on one end of a wooden splinter and heat in the reducing flame till the mass fuses. Dip the fused mass into sodium nitroprusside solution taken in a China dish.	Violet streaks are produced.
3. Lead acetate test To a part of aqueous solution of the salt add lead acetate solution.	A white ppt. is formed which is soluble in excess of hot ammonium acetate solution.

CONFIRMATION OF PHOSPHATE, PO$_4^{3-}$
(Not indicated in dilute and concentrated H$_2$SO$_4$ acid test).

Experiment	Observations
1. Ammonium molybdate test To the aqueous solution or sodium carbonate extract (or the original salt) add concentrated nitric acid and boil. Add ammonium molybdate solution in excess and again boil.	A deep yellow ppt. or coloration is obtained.
2. Magnesia mixture test Take a portion of aqueous solution (or a part of sodium carbonate extract, add hydrochloric acid to acidify it and boil off CO$_2$). Add magnesia mixture (to prepare it, add solid NH$_4$Cl to magnesium chloride solution. Boil, cool and add NH$_4$OH till a strong smell of ammonia is obtained) and allow to stand.	A white ppt. is obtained.

Chemical reactions involved in the confirmation of SO$_4^{2-}$ and PO$_4^{3-}$

SULPHATE $\left(SO_4^{2-}\right)$

1.   Barium chloride test

$$Na_2SO_4 + BaCl_2 \longrightarrow \underset{white}{BaSO_4} \downarrow + 2NaCl$$

2.   Match-stick test

$$Na_2SO_4 + BaCl_2 \longrightarrow BaSO_4 \downarrow + 2NaCl$$
$$BaSO_4 + Na_2CO_3 \longrightarrow Na_2SO_4 + BaCO_3$$
$$Na_2SO_4 + 4C \longrightarrow Na_2S + 4CO$$
$$Na_2S + Na_2[Fe(CN)_5NO] \longrightarrow \underset{Purple}{Na_4[Fe(CN)_5NOS]}$$

3.   Lead acetate test

$$Na_2SO_4 + Pb(CH_3COO)_2 \longrightarrow PbSO_4 \downarrow + 2CH_3COONa$$

PHOSPHATE $(PO_4{}^{3-})$

1.   Ammonium molybdate test

$$K_3PO_4 + \underset{Ammonium\ molybdate}{3(NH_4)_2MoO_4} \longrightarrow 2(NH_4)_3PO_4 + \underset{Pot.\ molybdate}{SK_2MoO_4}$$
$$K_2MoO_4 + 2HNO_3 \longrightarrow \underset{Molybdic\ acid}{H_2MoO_4} + 2KNO_3$$

$$H_2MoO_4 \longrightarrow MoO_3 + H_2O$$
$$(NH_4)_3PO_4 + 12MoO_3 + 6H_2O \longrightarrow (NH_4)_3PO_4 \cdot 12MoO_3 \cdot 6H_2O \downarrow$$

Ammonium phosphate molybdate (yellow ppt).

2.   Magnesia mixture test

$$Na_2HPO_4 + MgCl_2 + NH_4OH \longrightarrow \quad Mg(NH_4)PO_4 \downarrow + 2NaCl + H_2O.$$

Disodium   Mag. Ammonium
hydrogen   phosphate
phosphate   (white ppt.)

WET TESTS FOR BASIC (CATIONS)

Preliminary tests such as dry heating test, charcoal cavity test, flame test and borax bead test may give us some indication about the cation present in the salt. However, the cation is finally detected and confirmed through a systematic analysis involving wet tests. For the sake of qualitative analysis, the cations are Classified into the following groups (Table 12.10).

Table 12.10. Classification of Cations

Group	Cation
Group zero	$NH_4^+ Pb^{2+} Pb^{2+}, Cu^{2+} As^{3+}$
Group I	
Group IIA	
Group IIB	

Group	Cation
Group III	$Fe^{3+} Co^{2+}, Ni^{2+}, Mn^{2+}, Zn^{2+} Ba^{2+}, Sr^{2+}, Ca^{2+} Mg^{2+}$
Group IV	
Group V	
Group VI	

Before carrying out the wet tests for the analysis of cation, the salt has to be dissolved in some suitable solvent to prepare its solution.

PREPARATION OF SOLUTION FOR WET TESTS OF BASIC RADICALS

The very first essential step is to prepare a Clear and transparent solution of the salt under investigation. For this purpose, the under noted solvents are tried one after another in a systematic order. In case the salt does not dissolve in a particular solvent even on heating, try the next solvent. The following solvents are tried:

1. Distilled water (cold or hot).
2. Dilute HCl (cold or hot).
3. Cone. HCl (cold or hot).

PROCEDURE FOR THE PREPARATION OF SOLUTION

Take a small quantity of the given salt in a test tube. Add some suitable solvent into it and shake. If it does not dissolve even after heating for some time, take the fresh quantity of the salt again and treat it in a similar manner with next solvent. The Clear solution thus obtained is labelled as Original Solution (O.S.).

IMPORTANT NOTES

1. In case some gas is evolved during the preparation of solution, let the reaction cease. Gas must be completely expelled by heating.
2. In case solution is prepared in dilute HCl, group I is absent. Proceed with group II.
3. If the salt is soluble in hot water, and on cooling white precipitates appear, lead chloride is indicated.

4. It is necessary to dilute the solution if it is made in concentrated acid before proceeding with the analysis.

The following table will help the students in the choice of a suitable solvent:

Solvent	Salts which dissolve
1. Cold water	a) All NH_4^+, Na^+ and K^+ salts. b) All nitrites, nitrates and acetates. c) Most of the sulphates except those of Pb, Ba, Ca, Sr. d) All chlorides except that of lead.
2. Hot water	Lead chloride, lead nitrate.
3. Dil. HCl	All carbonates which do not dissolve in water i.e., Carbonates of Ca, Ba, Sr, Mg, Zn, Al, Cu, Ni, Mn, Fe etc., but not of Pb.

The separation of cations into various groups by making use of suitable reagents (known as group reagents) is based on the differences in chemical properties of cations. For example, if hydrochloric acid is added to a solution containing all cations, only the chlorides of lead, silver and mercury will precipitate, since all other chlorides are soluble. Thus, these cations form a group of ions which may be precipitated from solution by addition of group reagent HCl. Similarly, H_2S is a group reagent for group II. The following Table 12.11 Clearly shows the group reagents for different groups and the form in which cations of the particular group are precipitated out.

Table 12.11. Group Reagents

Group	Group reagent	Cations	Form in which cations are precipitated
Group zero	No	–	–
Group I	Dilute HCl	Pb^{2+}	Chlorides
Group II	H_2S in the presence of dilute HCl	Pb^{2+} Cu^{2+}, As^{3+}	Sulphides
Group III	NH_4OH in the presence of NH_4Cl	Fe^{3+}, Al^{3+}	Hydroxides
Group IV	H_2S in the presence of NH_4OH	Ni^{2+}, Mn^{2+}, Zn^{2+}, Co^{2+}	Sulphides
Group V	$(NH_4)_2CO_3$ in the presence of NH_4OH	Ca^{2+}, Ba^{2+}, Sr^{2+}	Carbonates
Group VI	No	Mg^{2+}	–

THEORY OF PRECIPITATION OF DIFFERENT GROUPS

The Classification of cations into different groups in the inorganic qualitative analysis is based upon the knowledge of solubility products of salts of these basic radicals. For example, chlorides of Hg_2^{2+}, Pb^{2+} and Ag^+ have very low solubility products.On the basis of this knowledge these radicals are grouped together in group-I and are precipitated as their chlorides by adding dilute HCl to their solutions. For adjusting the conditions for precipitation, another concept called common ion effect plays very important role. Before we consider the precipitation of radicals of other groups, let us discuss in brief the concept of common ion effect.

COMMON ION EFFECT

Weak acids and weak bases are ionised only to small extent in their aqueous solutions. In their solutions, unionised molecules are in dynamic equilibrium with ions. The degree of ionisation of a weak electrolyte (weak acid or weak base) is further suppressed if some strong electrolyte which can furnish some ion common with the ions furnished by weak electrolyte, is added to its solution. This effect is called common ion effect. For example, degree of ionisation of NH_4OH (a weak base) is suppressed by the addition of NH_4Cl (a strong electrolyte). The ionisation of NH_4OH and NH_4Cl in solution is represented as follows:

$$NH_4OH(aq) \rightleftharpoons \underset{\text{Common ion}}{NH_4^+(aq)} + OH^-(aq) \quad \text{... weakly ionised ... (12.1)}$$

$$NH_4Cl \rightarrow \underset{\text{Common ion}}{NH_4^+(aq)} + Cl^+(aq) \quad \text{... strongly ionised ... (12.2)}$$

Due to the addition of NH_4Cl, which is strongly ionised in the solution, concentration of NH_4 ions increase in the solution. Therefore, according to Le-Chatelier's principal equilibrium in equation (12.1) shifts in the backward direction in favor of unionised NH_4OH. In this way, addition of NH_4Cl suppresses the degree of ionisation of NH_4OH. Thus, the concentration of OH^- ions in the solution is considerably reduced and the weak base NH_4OH becomes a still weaker base.

The suppression of the degree of ionisation of a weak electrolyte (weak acid or weak base) by the addition of some strong electrolyte having a common ion, is called the common ion effect.

Application of concept of common ion effect in the qualitative analysis is illustrated as follows:

The cations of group II (Pb^{2+}, Cu^{2+}, AS^{3+}) are precipitated as their sulphides. Solubility products of sulphides of group II radicals are very low. Therefore, even with low concentration of S^{2-} ions, the ionic products (Qs_p) exceed the value of their solubility products (KS_p) and the radicals of group II get precipitated. The low concentration of S^{2-} ions is obtained by passing H_2S gas through the solution of the salts in the presence of dil. HCl which suppresses degree of ionisation of H_2S by common ion effect.

$$H_2S \rightleftharpoons 2H^+ + \underset{\text{Common ion}}{S^{2-}} \quad \text{...(12.3)}$$

$$HCl \longrightarrow \underset{\text{Common ion}}{H^+} + Cl \quad \text{...(12.4)}$$

It is necessary to suppress the concentration of S^{2-} ions, otherwise radicals of group IV will also get precipitated along with group II radicals.

Radicals of group IV (Ni^{2+}, CO^{2+}, Mn^{2+}, Zn^{2+}) are also precipitated as their sulphides. But solubility products of their sulphides are quite high. In order that ionic products exceed solubility products, concentration of S^{2-} ions should be high in this case. High concentration of sulphide ions is achieved by passing H_2S gas through the solutions of the salts in the presence of NH_4OH. Hydroxyl ions from NH_4OH combine with H^+ ions from H_2S. Due to the removal of H^+ ions the equilibrium of H_2S shifts in favor of ionised form.

$$\begin{aligned}
H_2S &\rightleftharpoons 2H^+ + S^{2-} \\
NH_4OH &\rightleftharpoons NH_4^+ + OH^- \\
H^+ + OH^- &\rightleftharpoons H_2O
\end{aligned}$$

Hence, concentration of S^{2-} ions increases. With this increased concentration of S^{2-} ions ionic products exceed solubility products and radicals of group IV get precipitated.

Radicals of group III (Fe^{3+}, Al^{3+}) are precipitated as their hydroxides by NH_4OH in the presence of NH_4Cl. The purpose of NH_4Cl is to suppress the degree of ionisation of NH_4OH by common ion effect in order to decrease the concentration of OH^- ions.

$$NH_4OH \rightleftharpoons \underset{\text{Common ion}}{NH_4^+} + OH^-$$

$$NH_4Cl \longrightarrow \underset{\text{Common ion}}{Cl_4^{\,+}} + Cl^-$$

The solubility products of hydroxides of group III radicals are quite low. Therefore, even with this suppressed concentration of OH^- ions their ionic products exceed solubility products and hence they get precipitated. If the concentration of OH^- ions is not suppressed, the radicals of groups IV, V and Mg_2^+ will also be precipitated along with radicals of group III.

Radicals of group V (Ba_2^+, Sa_2^+, Ca_2^+) are precipitated as their carbonates by the addition of $(NH_4)_2\,CO_3$ in the presence of NH_4Cl and NH_4OH. NH_4Cl suppresses the degree of ionisation of $(NH_4)_2\,CO_3$ by common ion effect and hence decreases the concentration of CO_3^{2-} ions.

$$(NH_4)_2CO_3 \rightleftharpoons \underset{\text{Common ion}}{2NH_4^+} + CO_3^{2-}$$

$$NH_4Cl \longrightarrow \underset{\text{Common ion}}{NH_4^+} + Cl^-$$

But solubility products of carbonates of group V radicals are quite low and hence even with the suppressed concentration of CO_3^{2-} ions their ionic products exceed solubility products, and they get precipitated whereas Mg^{2+} and other radicals of group VI having relatively high solubility products are not precipitated.

ANALYSIS OF GROUP ZERO (NH_4^+)

This group includes NH_4^+ cation. During the analysis of cations NH_4Cl and NH_4OH are added in many steps. Therefore, H_4^+ ion is detected in the beginning using solid salt.

PROCEDURE

The solid salt is heated with concentrated solution of sodium hydroxide. In case, ammonia gas is evolved, NH_4^+ is present. Evolution of NH_3 gas is confirmed by the following tests:

1. Characteristic ammoniacal smell.
2. The gas gives white fumes when a glass rod dipped in dil. HCl is brought near the mouth of the test tube.
3. When the gas is passed through Nessler's reagent, it would give brown ppt. in case of NH_3.

CHEMICAL REACTIONS INVOLVED IN GROUP-ZERO ANALYSIS

$$NH_4Cl + NaOH \xrightarrow{\Delta} NaCl + H_2O + NH_3 \uparrow$$
$$\underset{\text{White fumes}}{NH_3 + HCl \longrightarrow NH_4Cl}$$

NESSLER'S REAGENT TEST

$$\underset{\text{Nessler's Reagent}}{2K_2[HgI_4]} + NH_3 + 3KOH \longrightarrow \underset{\text{Brown ppt.}}{H_2N.HgO \cdot HgI \downarrow} + 7KI + 2H_2O$$

ANALYSIS OF GROUP I (SILVER GROUP)

This group includes Pb^{2+}, Ag^+ and Hg_2^{2+}. But in the present context, we shall study only Pb^{2+}. Group reagent for this group is dil. hydrochloric acid.

PROCEDURE

To the original solution add dil. hydrochloric acid. If a white precipitate is formed, first group (Pb^{2+}) is present. Filter and wash the ppt. with cold water and follow the instructions as given below:

ANALYSIS OF GROUP I (Pb^{2+})

Boil the white precipitate with $5 - 10ml$ of water. Precipitate dissolves. Divide the solution tained into three parts. Confirmation:

1   Cool one part of the solution under tap. White crystalline ppt. separates out.
2   Potassium iodide test. To the second part of the solution, add KI solution -yellow ppt.
3   Potassium chromate test. To the third part of the solution add K_2CrO_4 solution-yellow ppt.

CHEMICAL REACTIONS INVOLVED IN GROUP I ANALYSIS

The addition of HCl to the solution will precipitate Pb^{2+} as chloride

$$Pb(NO_3)_2 + 2HCl \longrightarrow PbCl_2 \downarrow + 2HNO_3$$
$$\text{White ppt.}$$

When the white ppt. is boiled with water, the precipitates dissolve because the $PbCl_2$ is soluble in hot water.

CONFIRMATORY TESTS

On cooling, precipitates settle down as $PbCl_2$ is less soluble in cold water.

1. Potassium iodide test

$$PbCl_2 + 2KI \longrightarrow PbI_2 \downarrow + 2KCl$$
$$\text{(Hot solution)} \qquad \text{Yellow ppt.}$$

2. Potassium chromate test

$$PbCl_2 + K_2CrO_4 \rightarrow PbCrO_4 \downarrow + 2KCl.$$
$$\text{(Hot solution)} \qquad \text{Yellow ppt.}$$

ANALYSIS OF GROUP II (COPPER GROUP)

This group inCludes Pb^{2+} and Cu^{2+} in IIA group and As^{3+} in IIB Group. These are precipitated as their sulphides. If group I is absent, the tests for radicals of group II are carried out. Group reagent for this group is H_2S gas in the presence of dil. HCl.

PROCEDURE

Take about 2 ml of the original solution in a test tube. Make it acidic with dil. HCl and warm the contents. Through this solution pass H_2S gas from the Kipp's apparatus by turning the stop cock as shown in Fig. 12.10, Formation of the black or yellow precipitates indicates the presence of group II radical. If this is observed, pass more of H_2S gas to ensure complete precipitation of the radical sulphide. Centrifuge and separate the precipitates.

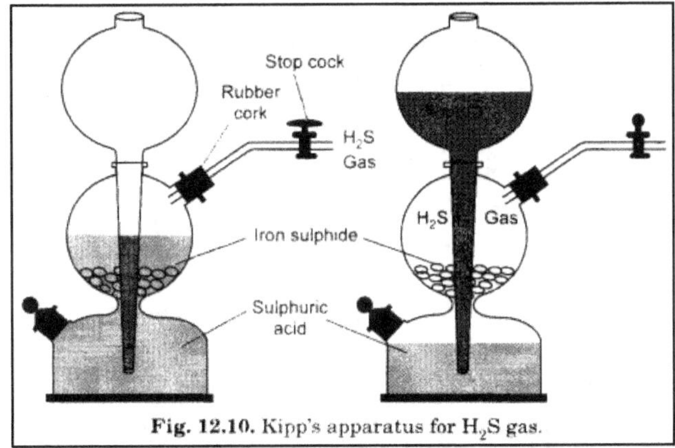

Fig. 12.10. Kipp's apparatus for H_2S gas.

Identification of IIA and IIB GroupS. Note the color of the precipitate. If the precipitate is black in color, it indicates Pb^{2+} or Cu^{2+}. If the color of precipitate is yellow this indicates As^{+3}

Table 12.13. Analysis of Group II

Black ppt. (Pb^{2+} or Cu^{2+}) Heat the black ppt. with minimum quantity $(1-2\ ml)$ of $50\%HNO_3$ ppt. dissolyes. To one part of the above solution, add dil. H_2SO_4 and alcohol.		**Yellow ppt. As^{+3}**
White ppt. (Pb^{2+}) Confirmation Dissolve the ppt. in hot ammonium acetate solution. Divide the solution into two parts: 1. Potassium iodide test To one part add pot. iodide solution. Yellow ppt. is formed. The ppt. dissolves in boiling water and on cooling recrystallises. 2. Potassium chromate test To another part add pot. chromate solution. Yellow ppt. is formed which dissolves in NaOH solution.	No white ppt. To rest of the solution add NH_4OH in excess Blue colored solution (Cu^{2+}) Confirmation 1. Potassium ferrocyanide test To one part of the blue solution add acetic acid and pot. ferrocyanide solution. A chocolate brown ppt. is formed. 2. Potassium iodide test To another part add acetic acid and pot. iodide solution. A white ppt. is formed in brown colored solution.	Confirmation Dissolve the yellow ppt. in conc. HNO_3 and divide it into two parts. 1. Ammonium molybdate test. To a part of the solution, add ammonium molybdate solution and heat-A yellow ppt. 2. Magnesia mixture test. Make the second part of the solution alkaline with NH_4OH solution and add magnesia mixture (contains solutions of $MgSO_4$, NH_4Cl and NH_4OH mixed in equal volumes)-A white ppt.

CHEMICAL REACTIONS INVOLVED IN THE ANALYSIS OF GROUP II

$$PbCl_2 + H_2S \longrightarrow 2HCl + PbS \downarrow \quad \text{(Black)}$$

$$CuCl_2 + H_2S \longrightarrow 2HCl + CuS \downarrow \quad (\text{Black})$$

$$2AsCl_3 + 3H_2S \longrightarrow 6HCl + As_2S_3 \downarrow \quad (\text{Yellow})$$

LEAD (Pb^{2+})

Black ppt. of PbS dissolves in 50% nitric acid. On adding sulfuric acid, lead sulphate precipitates.

$$3PbS + 8HNO_3 \longrightarrow 3Pb(NO_3)_2 + 4H_2O + 2NO + 3S$$

$$Pb(NO_3)_2 + H_2SO_4 \longrightarrow 2HNO_3 + PbSO_4 \downarrow$$
$$\text{(white)}$$

1. Potassium iodide test

$$Pb(NO_3)_2 + 2KI \longrightarrow 2KNO_3 + PbI_2 \downarrow$$
$$\text{(yellow)}$$

2. Potassium chromate test

$$Pb(NO_3)_2 + K_2CrO_4 \longrightarrow 2KNO_3 + PbCrO_4 \downarrow$$
$$\text{(yellow)}$$

COPPER (Cu^{2+})

Black ppt. of CuS dissolves in 50% nitric acid and a blue solution is obtained on a excess of NH_4OH.

$$3CuS + 8HNO_3 \longrightarrow 3Cu(NO_3)_2 + 4H_2O + 2NO + 3S$$
$$Cu(NO_3)_2 + 4NH_4OH \longrightarrow \underset{\text{(Blue solution)}}{[Cu(NH_3)_4][NO_3]_2} + 4H_2O$$

1. Potassium ferrocyanide test

$$[Cu(NH_3)_4]SO_4 + 4CH_3COOH \longrightarrow CuSO_4 + 4CH_3COONH_4$$
$$2CuSO_4 + K_4[Fe(CN)_6] \longrightarrow \underset{\text{(Chocolate brown color)}}{Cu_2[Fe(CN)_6] \downarrow} + 2K_2SO_4$$

2. Potassium iodide test

$$2CuSO_4 + 4KI \longrightarrow \underset{\substack{\text{White} \\ \text{ppt.}}}{Cu_2I_2 \downarrow} + \underset{\substack{\text{Brown} \\ \text{coloration}}}{I_2} + 2K_2SO_4$$

ARSENIC (As^{3+})

The yellow residue of As_2S_3 is dissolved in conc. HNO_3 forming arsenic acid.

$$As_2S_3 + 10HNO_3 \longrightarrow \underset{\text{Soluble}}{2H_3AsO_4} + 10NO_2 + 3S + 2H_2O$$

1. Ammonium molybdate test

$$H_3AsO_4 + 12(NH_4)_2MoO_4 + 21HNO_3 \longrightarrow \underset{\substack{\text{Yellow ppt. of ammonium} \\ \text{arseno molybdate}}}{(NH_4)_3AsO_4 \cdot 12MoO_3 \downarrow} + 21NH_4NO_3 + 12H_2O$$

2. Magnesia mixture test

$$H_3AsO_4 + MgSO_4 + 3NH_4OH \longrightarrow \underset{\text{White ppt.}}{Mg(NH_4)_2AsO_4} + (NH_4)_2SO_4 + 3H_2O$$

ANALYSIS OF GROUP III (IRON GROUP)

The cations present in this group are Fe^{2+}, Fe^{3+}, Cr^{3+} and Al^{3+}. Only Fe^{2+}/Fe^{3+} and Al^{3+} are included in the syllabus of this Class. These cations are precipitated as hydroxides by adding ammonium hydroxide in presence of ammonium chloride. Thus, group reagent for this group is NH_4OH in the presence of NH_4Cl.

PROCEDURE

In case, first and second groups are absent proceed for group III with the original solution. Take about 5 ml of the original solution and add 4-5 drops of cone, nitric acid. Boil the solution for some time. Add to it about 2 g of solid NH_4Cl and boil again. Cool the solution under tap water. Add excess of ammonium hydroxide to it and shake. A ppt. shows the presence of some cation of group III. Filter the ppt. and wash with water. Note the color of the ppt. If the ppt. is reddish brown in color, it indicates the presence of Fe^{3+} and if the color is white, it indicates the presence of Al^{3+}. Analyses the ppt. and draw inferences as in Table 12.14.

Table 12.14. Analysis of Group III (Fe^{3+} and Al^{3+})

Fe^{3+} (Reddish brown ppt.)	Al^{3+} (White ppt.)
Dissolve the reddish-brown ppt. in dilute HCl, and divide the solution into two parts.	
Confirmation 1. Potassium ferrocyanide test. To one part of the above solution add potassium ferrocyanide solution. Prussian blue coloration. 2. Potassium sulphocyanide test. To the second part, add a little potassium sulphocyanide solution. Blood red coloration.	**Confirmation** 1. Lake test. Dissolve the white ppt. in dilute hydrochloric acid. Add to it two drops of blue litmus solution. To this, add NH_4OH dropwise till blue color develops. Blue ppt. floating in the colorless solution. 2. Cobalt nitrate test. Perform charcoal cavity/Cobalt nitrate test with the salt. Blue mass.

Note:

1. Test of Fe^{2+}. The addition of cone, nitric acid in the analysis of group III serves to oxidise Fe^{2+} ions to Fe^{3+} ions. Add cone, nitric acid only if the cation is Fe^{2+} otherwise the addition of nitric acid may be avoided. To test this, add a few drops of potassium ferricyanide solution to the original salt solution. A deep blue colouration shows Fe^{2+}.

2. Use sufficient quantity of ammonium chloride, otherwise the hydroxides of higher group may be precipitated along with the radicals of third group.

3. Add NH_4OH until the solution gives the smell of ammonia.

Chemical Reactions Involved in the Analysis of Group III

The group III cations are precipitated as hydroxides on the addition of excess of ammonium hydroxide.

$$FeCl_3 + 3NH_4OH \longrightarrow 3NH_4Cl + Fe(OH) \downarrow$$
(Reddish brown ppt.)

$$AlCl_3 + 3NH_4OH \longrightarrow 3NH_4Cl + Al(OH)_3 \downarrow$$
(White ppt.)

IRON (Fe^{3+})

The reddish-brown ppt. of $Fe(OH)_3$ is dissolved in HCl.

$$Fe(OH)_3 + 3HCl \longrightarrow FeCl_3 + 3H_2O$$

1. Potassium ferrocyanide test

$$4FeCl_3 + 3K_4[Fe(CN)_6] \longrightarrow 12KCl + Fe_4[Fe(CN)_6]_3$$
Ferric ferrocyanide
(Prussian blue)

2. Potassium sulphocyanide test

$$FeCl_3 + 3KCNS \longrightarrow 3KCl + Fe(CNS)_3$$
Ferric sulphocyanide
(Blood red coloration)

ALUMINIUM (Al^{3+})

1. Lake test

$$Al(OH)_3 + 3HCl \longrightarrow AlCl_3 + 3H_2O \quad \text{...dissolution}$$

$$AlCl_3 + 3NH_4OH \longrightarrow 3NH_4Cl + \underset{\substack{\text{Blue color} \\ \text{adsorbs on this ppt.}}}{Al(OH)_3} \downarrow$$

ANALYSIS OF GROUP IV (ZINC GROUP)

The radicals present in this group are CO^{2+}, Ni^{2+}, Mn^{2+} and Zn^{2+}. These are precipitated as sulphides by passing H_2S gas through the ammoniacal solution of the salt.

The group reagent for this group is H_2S gas in the presence of NH_4Cl and NH_4OH.

PROCEDURE

If there is no ppt. in the third group, then use the same ammoniacal solution for the fourth group. Pass H_2S gas through the solution. If some ppt. is formed, presence of some radical of group IV is indicated. Filter the ppt. and wash it with water. Note the color of the ppt. and analyses the ppt. according to the Table 12.15.

Table 12.15. Analysis of Group IV Radicals (Co^{2+}, Ni^{2+}, Mn^{2+} and Zn^{2+})

Black ppt. (Co^{2+} or Ni^{2+}) Observe the color of the original salt. If the salt is purple or deep violet in color perform confirmatory tests for Co^{2+} and if it is greenish perform confirmatory tests for Ni^{2+} with the original solution.		Buff (flesh) colored ppt. Mn^{2+}	Dull white ppt. Zn^{2+}
Confirmation of Co^{2+} 1. Potassium nitride test To one part of the O.S. add ammonium hydroxide to neutralise the solution. Add acetic acid and a crystal of potassium nitrite. Warm. A yellow ppt. is formed. 2. Ammonium thiocyanate ether test To another part add ether (1 ml). Add a crystal of Ammonium thiocyanate, shake. Allow to settle. Blue color in ethereal layer confirms Co^{2+}. 3. Borax bead test Perform borax bead test with the salt. A blue bead is formed.	Confirmation of Ni^{2+} 1. Dimethyl glyoxime test To one part of O.S. add Ammonium hydroxide solution and few drops of dimethyl glyoxime. Bright rose red ppt. is obtained. 2. Sodium hydroxide Br_2 test To another part add sodium hydroxide (in excess) and bromine water Boil. A black ppt. is formed. 3. Borax bead test Perform borax bead test with the salt. Brown bead in oxidizing and grey bead in reducing flame is obtained.	Confirmation of Mn^{2+} 1. Sodium hydroxide Br_2 test To the O.S. add NaOH solution Shake. A white ppt. is formed. Add Br_2 water to white ppt. It turns black or brown. 2. Lead peroxide test To black ppt. obtained in above test add conc. HNO_3 and lead peroxide. Boil, cool and allow to settle. Pink-colored solution is formed. 3. Borax bead test Perform borax bead test with the salt. Pinkish bead in oxidizing flame and colorless bead in reducing flame.	Confirmation of Zn^{2+} 1. Sodium hydroxide. test To one part of O. S. add sodium hydroxide solution dropwise. A white ppt. is formed. Add more of NaOH. The white ppt. dissolves. 2. Pot. ferrocyanide test To another part, add pot. ferrocyanide solution White or bluish white ppt. is formed. 3. Charcoal Cavity/Cobalt Nitrite Test Perform Charcoal Cavity/Cobalt Nitrate test with the salt. Greenish residue is obtained.

CHEMICAL REACTIONS INVOLVED IN THE ANALYSIS OF GROUP IV

Passing of H_2S gas through the group III solution will precipitate the radicals CO^{2+}, Ni^{2+}, Mn^{2+} and Zn^{2+} as their sulphides. Formation of black ppt. (CoS or NiS) indicates cobalt or nickel. Formation of buff-colored ppt. (MnS) indicates manganese and dirty white ppt. (ZnS) indicts zinc.

$$
\begin{aligned}
Co(OH)_2 + H_2S &\longrightarrow 2H_2O + CoS\downarrow \quad \text{(Black)}\\
Ni(OH)_2 + H_2S &\longrightarrow 2H_2O + NiS\downarrow \quad \text{(Black)}\\
Zn(OH)_2 + H_2S &\longrightarrow 2H_2O + ZnS\downarrow \quad \text{(White)}\\
Mn(OH)_2 + H_2S &\longrightarrow 2H_2O + MnS\downarrow \quad \text{(Buff-colored)}
\end{aligned}
$$

COBALT (Co^{2+})

1. **Potassium nitrite test**

$$\underset{\text{(O.S)}}{CoCl_2} + 2KNO_2 \longrightarrow 2KCl + \underset{\text{Cobaltous nitrite}}{Co(NO_2)_2}$$

$$KNO_2 + CH_3COOH \longrightarrow CH_3COOK + HNO_2$$

$$Co(NO_2)_2 + 2HNO_2 \longrightarrow \underset{\text{cobaltic nitrite}}{Co(NO_2)_3} + H_2O + NO$$

$$Co(NO_2)_3 + 3KNO_2 \longrightarrow \underset{\substack{\text{Pot. cobalti nitrite}\\ \text{(yellow ppt.)}}}{K_3[Co(NO_2)_6]}$$

2. **Ammonium thiocyanate ether test**

   On addition of ether and a crystal of ammonium thiocyanate (shaking and allowing to stand), a blue color due to the formation of ammonium cobalt thiocyanate, is obtained in the ethereal layer.

$$CoCl_2 + 4NH_4CNS \longrightarrow (NH_4)_2[Co(CNS)_4] + 2NH_4Cl$$

NICKEL (Ni^{2+})

1. **Dimethyl glyoxime test: (with O:S.)**

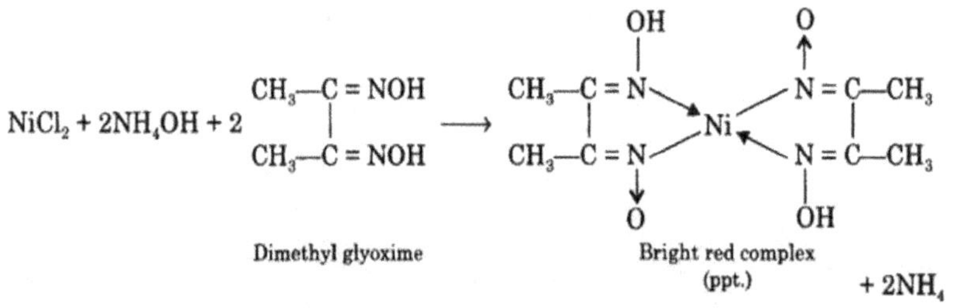

2. **Sodium hydroxide-bromine water test**

$$NiCl_2 + 2NaOH \longrightarrow 2NaCl + \underset{\text{(green ppt.)}}{Ni(OH)_2\downarrow}$$

$$Br_2 + H_2O \longrightarrow 2HBr + [O]$$

$$2Ni(OH)_2 + H_2O + [O] \longrightarrow \underset{\substack{\text{Nickelic hydroxide}\\ \text{(Black ppt.)}}}{2Ni(OH)_3\downarrow}$$

MANGANESE (Mn^{2+})

Manganese sulphides dissolves in dil. HCl forming manganese chloride, and H_2S is boiled off.

$$MnS + 2HCl \longrightarrow MnCl_2 + H_2S\uparrow$$

1. NaOH and Br$_2$ water test

$$MnCl_2 + 2NaOH \longrightarrow Mn(OH)_2 \downarrow + 2NaCl$$
$$\text{White ppt.}$$

The white ppt. of manganese hydroxide turns brown on adding Br$_2$ water due to its oxidation to brown manganic hydroxide MnO(OH)$_2$

$$Br_2 + H_2O \longrightarrow 2HBr + [O]$$
$$Mn(OH)_2 + [O] \longrightarrow MnO(OH)_2 \downarrow$$
$$\text{Brown ppt.}$$

2. PbO$_2$ test

$$MnS + 2HNO_3 \longrightarrow Mn(NO_3)_2 + H_2S$$
$$2Mn(NO_3)_2 + 5PbO_2 + 6HNO_3 \longrightarrow 2HMnO_4 + 5Pb(NO_3)_2 + 2H_2O$$
$$\text{Pink solution}$$

ZINC (Zn^{2+})

The precipitate of ZnS obtained in Group IV is white.
The white ppt. of ZnS dissolves in dil. HCl, and H$_2$S is boiled off.

$$ZnS + 2HCl \longrightarrow ZnCl_2 + H_2S \uparrow$$

1. NaOH test

$$ZnCl_2 + 2NaOH \longrightarrow Zn(OH)_2 \downarrow + 2NaCl$$
$$\text{White ppt.}$$
$$Zn(OH)_2 + 2NaOH \longrightarrow Na_2ZnO_2 + 2H_2O$$
$$\text{White ppt.} \qquad\qquad \text{Solute}$$

2. Potassium ferrocyanide test

$$2ZnCl_2 + K_4[Fe(CN)_6] \longrightarrow Zn_2[Fe(CN)_6] \downarrow + 4KCl$$
$$\text{White Bluish-}$$
$$\text{white ppt.}$$

ANALYSIS OF GROUP V (CALCIUM GROUP)

Group V consists of three radicals: Ba^{2+}, Sr^{2+} and Ca^{2+}. These cations are precipitated as their carbonates. Group reagent for this group is (NH$_4$)$_2$CO$_3$ in the presence of NH$_4$Cl and NH$_4$OH.

PROCEDURE

If the fourth group is absent, then proceed for radicals of group V.
To the O.S. add 2-3 gins of solid NH$_4$Cl, boil, cool and add NH$_4$OH till the solution smells of ammonia. Then add (NH$_4$)$_2$CO$_3$ solution. Appearance of white ppt. indicates the presence of group V cation. Filter and wash the ppt. with water. Dissolve the ppt. in hot dil. acetic acid. Divide the solution into three parts and proceed as in Table 12.16.

Table 12.16. Analysis of Group V(Ba^{2+}, Sr^{2+}, Ca^{2+})

Ba^{2+}	Sr^{3+}	Ca^{2+}
1. Potassium chromate test To one part of the solution, add a few drops of potassium chromate solution. Yellow ppt. 2. Flame test Perform flame test with the original salt. Grassy green flame.	Test for Sr^{2+} only if Ba^{2+} is absent. 1. Ammonium sulphate test To the second part of the solution, add 1ml of Ammonium sulphate solution and warm. White ppt. 2. Flame test Perform flame test with the original salt. Crimson red flame.	Test for Ca^{2+} only if Ba^{2+} and Sr^{2+} are absent. 1. Ammonium oxalate test To the third portion of the solution, add 1-2 ml of Ammonium oxalate solution. Add a little Ammonium hydroxide to it and scratch the sides. White ppt. 2. Flame test Perform flame test with the original salt. Brick red flame.

Note:
1. *Proceed to test for group V cations in the order, Ba^{2+}, Sr^{2+} and Ca^{2+}. If Ba^{2+} is confirmed, do not test for Sr^{2+} or Ca^{2+} Similarly if Sr^{2+} is confirmed, do not test for Ca^{2+}.*
2. *Original solution can be preferably used for testing Sr^{2+} and Ca^{2+}.*

CHEMICAL REACTIONS INVOLVED IN THE ANALYSIS OF GROUP V RADICALS

When $(NH_4)_2CO_3$ is added to a salt solution containing NH_4Cl and NH_4OH, the Ba^{2+}, Sr^{2+} and Ca^{2+} are precipitated.

$$BaCl_2 + (NH_4)_2CO_3 \longrightarrow BaCO_3 \downarrow + 2NH_4Cl$$
$$SrCl_2 + (NH_4)_2CO_3 \longrightarrow SrCO_3 \downarrow + 2NH_4ClCaCl_2 + (NH_4)_2CO_3 \longrightarrow CaCO_3 \downarrow + 2NH_4Cl$$

This insoluble carbonate dissolves in acetic acid due to formation of soluble Barium.

BARIUM (Ba^{2+})

White ppt. of $BaCO_3$ dissolves in hot dilute acetic acid.

$$BaCO_3 + 2CH_3COOH \longrightarrow (CH_3COO)_2Ba + CO_2 \downarrow + H_2O$$

1. Potassium chromate test

$$(CH_3COO)_2Ba + K_2CrO_4 \longrightarrow 2CH_3COOK + BaCrO_4 \downarrow$$
(yellow ppt.)

2. Flame test

Barium imparts grassy green color to the flame.

Strontium (Sr^{2+})

White ppt. of $SrCO_3$ dissolves in hot dilute acetic acid.

$$SrCO_3 + 2CH_3COOH \longrightarrow (CH_3COO)_2Sr + CO_2 \uparrow + H_2O$$

1. **Ammonium sulphate test**

$$(CH_3COO)_2Sr + (NH_4)_2SO_4 \longrightarrow 2CH_3COONH_4 + \underset{\text{(white ppt.)}}{SrSO_4 \downarrow}$$

2. **Flame test**
Strontium produces crimson red flame.

Calcium (Ca^{2+})
White ppt. of $CaCO_3$ dissolves in hot dil. acetic acid.

$$CaCO_3 + 2CH_3COOH \longrightarrow (CH_3COO)_2Ca + CO_2 \uparrow + H_2O$$

1. **Ammonium oxalate test**

$$(CH_3COO)_2Ca + (NH_4)_2C_2O_4 \longrightarrow 2CH_3COONH_4 + \underset{\text{(white ppt.)}}{CaC_2O_4 \downarrow}$$

2.Flame test
Calcium imparts brick red color to the flame.

When $(NH_4)_2CO_3$ is added to a salt solution containing NH_4Cl and NH_4OH, the carbonates of Ba^{2+}, Sr^{2+} and Ca^{2+} are precipitated.

ANALYSIS OF GROUP VI (Mg^{2+})
1. **Ammonium phosphate test**
To a part of the original solution add some solid NH_4Cl and NH_4OH in slight excess. Then add ammonium phosphate solution and rub the sides of the test-tube with a glass rod.
A white ppt. confirms Mg^{2+}.

2. **Charcoal cavity cobalt nitrate test**
Perform charcoal cavity cobalt nitrate test with the original salt.
A pink mass is obtained.

AMMONIUM PHOSPHATE TEST
Chemical Reactions Involved in Confirmation of Mg^{2+}

$$MgCl_2 + NH_4OH + (NH_4)_2HPO_4 \longrightarrow Mg(NH_4)PO_4 \downarrow + 2NH_4Cl + H_2$$

Question.1. What do you mean by qualitative and quantitative analysis?

Answer. Qualitative analysis deals with the identification of mere presence of acidic or basic radicals in inorganic salts or presence of extra elements such as N, O, P, S or halogens in an organic compound or testing the presence of functional group in an organic compound.

Quantitative analysis on the other hand helps to estimate the amount/concentration/percentage of these elements present.

Question.2. Give an example to differentiate between qualitative and quantitative analysis.

Answer. When a given salt e.g., lead salt is analyses say with KI; appearance of yellow ppt. will indicate the qualitative presence of lead ions but in case if an alloy containing lead is dissolved in nitric acid and the amount of lead present is estimated by weighing the exact amount of lead iodide precipitated to calculate the percentage of lead in the alloy; it will be called as quantitative analysis.

Question.3. What is a radical?

Answer. An atom or a group of atoms having a distinct positive or negative charge on it is called a radical; for example, $NH_4^+, Cu^{+2}, Br^-, SO_4^{2-}$ etc.

Question.4. What is the color of iron salts?

Answer. Ferrous salts are generally green and ferric salts are brown.

Question.5. What is the color of nickel salts?

Answer. Bluish green or green.

Question.6. Give one example of red salt.

Answer. Cobalt nitrate is red in color.

Question.7. Generally, what is the color of manganese salts?

Answer. Light pink or flesh colored.

Question.8. What are deliquescent salts?

Answer. Salts which absorb moisture from the atmosphere and dissolve in it are called deliquescent salts e.g., $MgCl_2, FeCl_3, ZnCl_2$.

Question.9. What are efflorescent salts?

Answer. Salts which give out water of crystallisation are termed as efflorescent salts e.g., $FeSO_4 . 7H_2O$ or $Na_2CO_3 \cdot 10H_2O$ loses water of crystallisation to become $FeSO_4 x H_2O (3 < x < 7)$ and $Na_2CO_3 . H_2O$ (on losing 9 molecules of water of crystallisation).

Question.10. What is sublimation?

Answer. Sublimation is a process by which a salt directly changes its state from solid to gaseous without melting on heating. On cooling, the vapors condense to give back the solid.

Question.11. What do you mean by the term decrepitation?

Answer. Some salts that do not contain any water of crystallisation contain some mother liquor entrapped in their crystals during crystallisation.

On heating, these trapped molecules (liquid) of mother liquor escape producing crackling sound called decrepitation. Some examples of such salts are; $Ba(NO_3)_2, NaCl, Pb(NO_3)_2$

Question.12. Why are silver nitrate and hydrogen peroxide solutions kept in colored bottles?

Answer. Because they can get decomposed when exposed to light.

Question.13. Why do blue crystals of copper sulphate become colorless on heating?

Answer. Because the blue colored hydrated copper sulphate ($CuSO_4 . 5H_2O$) loses its water of crystallisation on heating and become colorless anhydrous copper sulphate.

$$CuSO_4 . 5H_2O \xrightarrow{\text{Heat}} CuSO_4 + 5H_2O$$

(Blue)   (Colorless)
hydraded copper   anhydrous copper
sulphate   sulphate

Question.14. Name the type of salt which produces a pale brown gas on heating.

Answer. Nitrate or Nitrite salts of metals.

Question.15. What information do you get when addition of dil. H_2SO_4 for testing acid radicals result in the formation of white precipitate?

Answer. It indicates that the cations present in the salt may be $Pb^{2+}, Ba^{2+}, Sr^{2+}$ or Ca^{2+} which form insoluble sulphates.

Question.16. While performing H_2SO_4 test, why should the reaction mixture not be heated to boiling?
Answer. On boiling, H_2SO_4 itself gets decomposed to give SO_2 which interferes with the identification of other gases evolved during the test.

Question.17. In case dil. H_2SO_4 interferes in test of acid radicals due to formation of precipitate of sulphate, how will you perform preliminary test for acid radicals?
Answer. The test can be performed by using HCl.

Question.18. Name the acid radicals that can be detected by conc. H_2SO_4 test.
Answer. $Cl^-, Br^-, I^-, CH_3COO^-, NO_3^-, C_2O_4^{2-}$.

Question.19. What is the function of copper piece or paper pellet when a nitrate is heated with conc. H_2SO_4?
Answer. When a nitrate salt is heated with conc. H_2SO_4, colorless vapors of HNO_3 are evolved. But when a paper pellet or Cu chips are added, carbon present in the paper or copper from copper chips reduce HNO_3 to NO_2 gas and brown fumes will be observed.

Question.20. How do you test for a sulphide ion?
Answer. H_2S gas having rotten egg smell is evolved when a sulphide salt is treated with dil. H_2SO_4. Further, H_2S gas evolved turns moist lead acetate paper black.

Question.21. Why does NO_2 turn $FeSO_4$ solution black?
Answer. $FeSO_4$ first reduces NO_2 to NO which then combines with $FeSO_4$ to form black colored nitroso ferrous sulphate.

$$2FeSO_4 + H_2SO_4 + NO_2 \longrightarrow Fe_2(SO_4)_3 + H_2O + NO$$
$$FeSO_4 + NO \longrightarrow FeSO_4 \cdot NO$$

Question.22. What is the need for preparing sodium carbonate extract?
Answer. Sodium carbonate extract is prepared to test the presence of anions when the salt is insoluble in water. On reacting with sodium carbonate, anion forms sodium salt of itself, thus, comes to solution, making its identification possible.

Question.23. Why is it necessary to neutralise sodium carbonate extract before testing for $SO_4^{(2-)}$ ion?
Answer. Sodium carbonate extract contains $CO_3^{\ 2}$ ions. If these are not decomposed with dil. HCl, white ppt. of $BaCO_3$ can be obtained on addition of $BaCl_2$ (even in absence of SO_4^{2-}), thereby of $BaCl_2$ (even in absence of SO_2^{2-}), thereby interfering in the identification of SO_4^{2-} ion.

Question.24. What is the chemical equation involved in the preparation of sodium carbonate extract?
Answer. $Na_2CO_3 + 2MA \longrightarrow M_2CO_3 + 2NaA$
(MA = Metal salt).

Question.25. Why treatment of a chloride with conc. H_2SO_3 liberates HCl while a bromide and iodide ion give bromine and iodine gas respectively?
Answer. Conc. H_2SO_4 acts as a weak oxidising agent hence HI and HBr produced during reaction of H_2SO_4 and I^- or Br^- get oxidised to I_2 and Br_2. However, conc. H_2SO_4 cannot oxidise HCl to Cl_2.

Question.26. What is the formula of the compound formed in ammonium molybdate test of O_4^{3-} ?
Answer. Yellow ppt. is formed due to the formation of ammonium phosphomolybdate $(NH_4)_3PO_4. 12MoO_3 \cdot 6H_2O$ (Yellow ppt.)

Question.27. Why is original solution prepared in water or HCl; and solid salt is not directly used for identification of basic radicals?
Answer. Since the identification is based on tests from solutions, the solid must be dissolved in either water or HCl to form solution. Also, most of the metal chlorides except first group are water soluble, hence HCl can be used to make O.S.

Question.28. Why H_2SO_4 cannot be used for making original solution?
Answer. Since H_2SO_4 will result in formation of sulphates of cations and most of the sulphates are insoluble in water, we cannot use H_2SO_4 for making original solution.

Question.29. Why is HNO_3 not used for making original solution?
Answer. HNO_3 is an oxidising agent and when H_2S is passed for group II and IV radicals, it gets oxidised to S and will interfere in analysis?

Question.30. Name the anions detected by conc. H_2SO_4.
Answer. Cl^-, Br^-, I^-, CH_3COO^- and NO_3^-.

Question.31. What is lime water and what happens on passing carbon dioxide gas through it?
Answer. Lime water is a solution of calcium hydroxide $[Ca(OH)_2]$. It turns milky on passing CO_2 gas through it due to the formation of white precipitate of insoluble calcium carbonate.

Question.32. Carbon dioxide gas and sulphur dioxide gas both turn lime water milky. How will you distinguish between the two?
Answer. On passing through acidified $K_2Cr_2O_7$ solution, SO_2 turns $K_2Cr_2O_7$ green while CO_2 shows no effect.

Question.33. How will you test the presence of carbonate ion?
Answer. On treating the mixture with dil. HCl, CO_2 gas is evolved. When the gas is passed through lime water. it turns milky.

$$Na_2CO_3 + 2HCl \longrightarrow 2NaCl + H_2O + CO_2 \uparrow$$

Question.34. Can we use ammonium sulphate instead of ammonium chloride in group III?
Answer. No, ammonium sulphate cannot be used in place of NH_4Cl in group III because it would cause precipitation of group V radicals as their sulphates in group III.

Question.35. Why is NH_4OH added before $(NH_4)_2CO_3$ solution while precipitating group V cations?
Answer. $(NH_4)_2CO_3$ contains some NH_4HCO_3 in it. NH_4OH is added to convert NH_4HCO_3 to $(NH_4)_2CO_3$ so that Ba^{2+}, Sr^{2+} and Ca^{2+} can be completely precipitated.

Question.36. What is aqua-regia?
Answer. It is a mixture of conc. HCl and conc. HNO_3 in the ratio of $3:1$ by volume.

Question.37. Name a cation, which is not obtained from a metal.
Answer. Ammonium ion (NH_4^+).

Question.38. How can you test the presence of ammonium ion?
Answer. Add NaOH to the salt and heat it. If NH_3 gas evolves, NH_4^+ ion is present. Pass this gas through Nessler's reagent, a brownish precipitate or coloration is observed.

Question.39. Why a salt containing lead turn black in color, if kept in laboratory for a long time?
Answer. It happens due to the formation of black lead sulphide by the action of H₂S in the atmosphere.

Question.40. What is the color of nickel and manganese salts?
Answer. Nickel salts are bluish green/green in color. Manganese salts are light pink/flesh in color.

DETECTION OF ELEMENTS IN ORGANIC COMPOUNDS

Detection of elements present in an organic compound constitutes an important step in its analysis. All the organic compounds contain carbon. Hydrogen is also present in most of the organic compounds (the few exceptions are the compounds such as CCl_4, CS_2, etc.). In addition to carbon and hydrogen other elements which are generally present in organic compounds are oxygen, nitrogen, sulphur and halogens.

Since nearly all the organic compounds contain carbon as well as hydrogen it is usually not necessary to carry out tests to detect them and their presence can be assumed without testing for them. Here, we shall study the tests for the detection of nitrogen, sulphur and halogens only.

AIM

Detection of Nitrogen, Sulphur, Chlorine, Bromine and Iodine by Lassaigne's Test

This is the most dependable test for the detection of nitrogen, Sulphur and halogens. This test is also known as sodium fusion test. In order to perform this test, first of all sodium extract or Lassaigne's extract is prepared as described below:

PREPARATION OF LASSAIGNE'S EXTRACT

Take a small piece of dry sodium in a fusion tube. Heat the tube slightly so that it melts to a shining globule. Add a pinch of the organic compound. Heat it slowly to start with so that the compound reacts with sodium metal. Now heat it strongly. Plunge the red-hot tube into a China dish containing distilled water. Crush the contents with a glass rod and heat to boiling. Remove the insoluble matter by filtration. The filtrate is called Lassaigne's extract.

Nitrogen, Sulphur and halogens present in an organic compound are detected by making use of Lassaigne's extract.

DETECTION OF NITROGEN

To a small portion of Lassaigne's extract (usually alkaline), add 2 ml of freshly prepared ferrous sulphate solution and heat. Now add to it 2-3 drops of ferric chloride solution and acidify with cone, hydrochloric acid. A Prussian blue coloration indicates the presence of nitrogen in the compound.

CHEMISTRY OF THE TEST

If nitrogen is present in the compound, the sodium extract would contain sodium cyanide formed during fusion. On adding the required reagents, sodium cyanide reacts to form Ferric-Ferro cyanide which has Prussian blue color.

OBSERVATIONS

Solution in Burette = HCl, Solution in pipette = Na_2CO_3, Indicator = Methyl orange, Color change = Yellow to light pink

The volume of the pipette = 10 ml

$$Na + \underset{\substack{\text{(From} \\ \text{organic} \\ \text{compund)}}}{C + N} \xrightarrow{\text{Fuse}} NaCN$$

$$FeSO_4 + 2NaOH \longrightarrow \underset{\text{Green ppt.}}{Fe(OH)_2 \downarrow} + Na_2SO_4$$

$$Fe(OH)_2 + \underset{\substack{\text{(From} \\ \text{sodium} \\ \text{extract)}}}{NaCN} \longrightarrow Fe(CN)_2 + 2NaOH$$

$$Fe(CN)_2 + 4NaCN \longrightarrow Na_4[Fe(CN)_6]$$
$$\text{Sod. ferrocyanide}$$

$$3Na_4[Fe(CN)_6] + 4FeCl_3 \longrightarrow Fe_4[Fe(CN_6]_3 + 12NaCl$$
$$\text{Ferric ferrocyanide}$$
$$\text{(prussian blue color)}$$

S. No.	Burette Readings		Volume of HCl used (ml)
	Initial reading	Final reading	

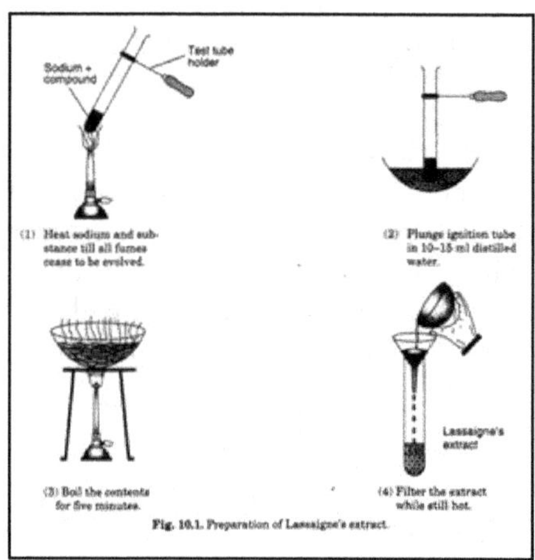

Fig. 10.1. Preparation of Lassaigne's extract.

purpose of acidifying the reaction mixture in the end is to dissolve any green ppt. of Fe (OH)$_2$ since it may lead to wrong inferences.

NITROGEN AND SULPHUR PRESENT TOGETHER

If the organic compound contains both nitrogen and Sulphur, sodium sulphocyanide (NaCNS) is formed during preparation of Lassaigne's extract. Sodium sulphocyanide reacts with ferric chloride and gives blood red coloration due to formation of ferric sulphocyanide.

$$Na + C + N + S \longrightarrow NaCNS$$
$$\text{From}$$
$$\text{organic}$$
$$\text{compound}$$

$$3NaCNS + FeCl_3 \longrightarrow Fe(CNS)_3 + 3NaCl$$
$$\text{Blood red}$$
$$\text{coloration}$$

Thus, appearance of a blood red coloration on performing Lassaigne's test for nitrogen indicates the presence of both nitrogen and Sulphur in the organic compound.

DETECTION OF SULPHUR

SODIUM NITROPRUSSIDE TEST

To a small portion of Lassaigne's extract add a few drops of sodium nitroprusside solution. A purple coloration indicates the presence of Sulphur in the compound.

CHEMISTRY OF THE TEST

During preparation of Lassaigne's extract Sulphur from the organic compound combines with sodium to form sodium supplied. Sulphides give purple coloration on reaction with sodium nitroprusside.

$$2Na + \underset{\substack{\text{(From} \\ \text{organic} \\ \text{Compund)}}}{S} \xrightarrow{\text{Fuse}} Na_2S$$

$$\underset{\substack{\text{(From} \\ \text{Sodium} \\ \text{extract)}}}{Na_2S} + \underset{\text{Sod. nitroprusside}}{Na_2[Fe(CN)_5NO]} \longrightarrow \underset{\text{Purple coloration}}{Na_4[Fe(CN)_5NOS]}$$

LEAD ACETATE TEST

Acidify a small portion of Lassaigne's extract with acetic acid and add a few drops of lead acetate solution. The formation of black ppt. indicates the presence of Sulphur in the compound.

CHEMISTRY OF THE TEST

$$Na_2S + (CH_3COO)_2Pb \longrightarrow \underset{\substack{\text{Black} \\ \text{ppt.}}}{PbS} \downarrow + 2CH_3COONa$$

DETECTION OF CHLORINE, BROMINE, AND IODINE

SILVER NITRATE TEST

To a small portion about 2 ml of Lassaigne's extract add 1 ml of cone, nitric acid and boil for some time. Cool the contents and add to it silver nitrate solution.

a) **White precipitate, soluble in ammonium hydroxide**, indicates the presence of chlorine in the organic compound.
b) **Pale yellow precipitate, sparingly soluble in ammonium hydroxide**, indicates the presence of bromine in the compound.
c) **Yellow precipitate, insoluble in ammonium hydroxide**, indicates the presence of iodine in the organic compound.

CHEMISTRY OF THE TEST

(a) For Chlorine

$$Na + \underset{\substack{\text{(From org.} \\ \text{compound}}}{Cl} \xrightarrow{\text{Heat}} NaCl$$

$$NaCl + AgNO_3 \longrightarrow \underset{\substack{\text{Silver chloride} \\ \text{(White ppt.)}}}{AgCl} \downarrow + NaNO_3$$

$$AgCl + 2NH_4OH \longrightarrow \underset{\text{(Soluble)}}{[Ag(NH_3)_2]Cl} + 2H_2O$$

(b) For Bromine

$$Na + \underset{\substack{\text{(From org.} \\ \text{compound)}}}{Br} \xrightarrow{\text{Heat}} NaBr$$

$$NaBr + AgNO_3 \longrightarrow \underset{\substack{\text{Silver bromide} \\ \text{(Pale yellow ppt.)}}}{AgBr \downarrow} + NaNO_3$$

(c) For Iodine

$$Na + \underset{\substack{\text{(From org.} \\ \text{compound)}}}{I} \xrightarrow{\text{Heat}} NaI$$

$$NaI + AgNO_3 \longrightarrow \underset{\substack{\text{Silver} \\ \text{iodide} \\ \text{(Yellow ppt.)}}}{AgI \downarrow} + NaNO_3$$

The function of adding cone. HNO_3 and boiling is to decompose any sodium cyanide or sodium supplied present in the extract. Otherwise, these compounds will interfere with the tests of halides since NaCN gives a white ppt. with silver nitrate while Na_2S gives a black ppt.

$$NaCN + HNO_3 \longrightarrow NaNO_3 + HCN \uparrow \quad Na_2S + 2HNO_3 \longrightarrow 2NaNO_3 + H_2S \uparrow$$

CARBON DISULPHIDE TEST

Acidify a small portion of Lassaigne's extract with dil. HCl and add a few drops of carbon disulphide (or CCl_4 or $CHCl_3$). Now add freshly prepared chlorine water and shake vigorously.

(a) Appearance of **orange color** in the carbon disulphide layer indicates the presence of **bromine**.

(b) Appearance of **violet color** in the carbon disulphide layer indicates the presence of **iodine**.

CHEMISTRY OF THE TEST

Chlorine can displace bromine and iodine from their respective halides in solution. Bromine or iodine thus liberated can turn the carbon disulphide layer orange or violet.

$$Cl_2 + \underset{\text{(From sodium}}{2NaBr} \rightarrow Br_2 + 2NaCl$$

$$Cl_2 + 2NaI \longrightarrow \underset{\text{(From sodiu extract)}}{I_2} + 2NaCl$$

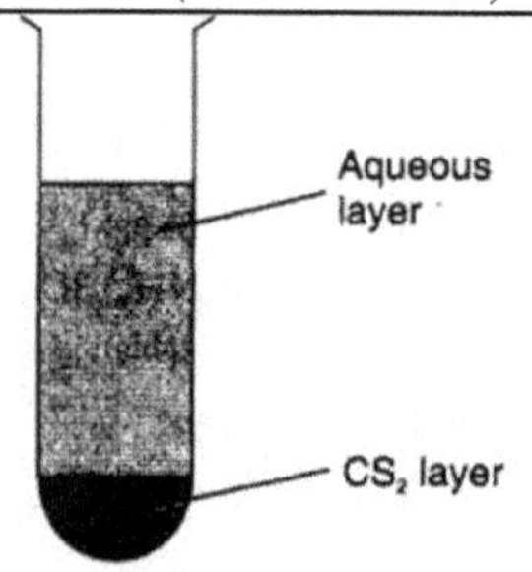

Fig. 10.2. Carbon disulphide test.

Table 10.1. Detection of N, S, Cl, Br and I by Lassaigne's Test

Experiment	Observations	Inference
Preparation of Lassaigne's extract Fuse a small piece of sodium in a fusion tube. Add a little organic compound to it and heat. Plunge it in a China dish containing distilled water. Boil the contents and filter. The filtrate is called Lassaigne's extract. 1. **Test for Nitrogen** To 2 ml of Lassaigne's extract add 2 ml of freshly prepared $FeSO_4$, boil and add a few drops of $FeCl_3$ solution and concentrated hydrochloric acid.	Prussian blue color	Nitrogen present
2. **Test for Sulphur** (a) To 2 ml of Lassaigne's extract add 2-3 drops of acetic acid and 1 ml of **lead acetate solution**. (b) To 2 ml of Lassaigne's extract add a few drops of **sodium nitroprusside solution**.	Black ppt. Purple color	Sulphur present Sulphur present
3. **Test for Halogens** (a) **Silver nitrate test** Acidify a little of Lassaigne's extract with concentrated HNO_3 boil, cooled and add silver nitrate solution. (b) **Carbon disulphide test** Acidify another portion of Lassaigne's extract with dil. HCl and add 1 ml of CS_2 and two drops of chlorine water and shake.	(i) **A curdy white ppt.** soluble in excess of NH_4OH. (ii) **A pale-yellow ppt.** sparingly soluble in NH_4OH. (iii) **A bright yellow ppt.** insoluble in NH_4OH. (i) **Orange color** in CS_2 layer. (ii) **Violet color** in CS_2 layer.	Chlorine present Bromine present Iodine present Bromine present Iodine present

Question.1. What is Lassaigne's extract?
Answer. Lassaigne's extract is prepared by fusing the organic compound with sodium metal and the fused product is then extracted with water. The extract so obtained is called L.E. or sodium extract.

Question.2. Why is sodium kept under kerosene?
Answer. Sodium metal reacts with oxygen and moisture present in air, hence kept under kerosene which prevents it's coming in contact with air.

Question.3. Can we use potassium in place of sodium in L.E.?
Answer. No, potassium is too reactive metal, hence dangerous to use.

Question.4. What are extra elements present in an organic compound? Why are they said so?
Answer. Organic compounds generally contain C and H. Other elements than these present in an organic compound are called extra elements. They are S, P, N, O and halogens.

Question.5. What is the purpose of fusion of organic compound with sodium metal for the preparation of L.E.?
Answer. When the organic compound is heated with sodium, the element such as nitrogen, sulphur and halogens if present in the compound are converted into sodium salts which are soluble in water. The aqueous solution is then used to identify these elements.

Question.6. How is sodium extract prepared?
Answer. Sodium extract is prepared by fusing the organic compound with sodium metal. This fused product is further extracted with water. The extract finally formed is known as sodium extract.
Nitrogen - urea
Sulphur - thiourea
Chlorine – chloroform

Question.7. If we use potassium in the place of sodium in sodium extract, what will happen?
Answer. Since, potassium is more reactive metal, so we cannot use it because it is very dangerous to use.

Question.8. In the Lassaigne's test for nitrogen, why bluish green color appears?

Ans When few drops of $FeCl_3$ solution is added to warm the solution of sodium extract and $FeSO_4$ solution, ferric ferrocyanide $Fe_4[Fe(CN)_6]_3$ is formed which gives bluish green color.

Question.9. In the test of sulphur, why violet color appears?
Answer. Because there is a formation of $Na_4[Fe(CN)_5NOS]$ which gives violet color at glance.

Question.10. Why CS_2 layer is colored in the test of detecting halogen?
Answer. Because Br_2 and I_2 have covalent bonding and hence, are more soluble in organic solvent CS_2 than in water. Thus CS_2 layer is colored.

Question.11. Why is L.E. usually alkaline?
Answer. Because during fusion, some sodium is generally left unreacted. This extra sodium when reacts with water forms NaOH solution which is basic in nature.

Question.12. Why is only distilled water used for preparing L.E.?
Answer. Tap water contains chloride ions, hence only distilled water is recommended.

Question.13. Why is freshly prepared ferrous sulphate solution used to test for nitrogen?
Answer. Because $FeSO_4$ solution on keeping gets oxidised to basic ferric sulphate by atmospheric oxygen.
$$4FeSO_4 + O_2 + 2H_2O \longrightarrow 4Fe(OH)SO_4$$
$$\underset{\text{sulphate}}{\text{Ferrous}} \qquad\qquad \underset{\substack{\text{ferric} \\ \text{sulphate}}}{\text{Basic}}$$
Consequently Fe^{2+} ions needed for the test are not available, hence freshly prepared $FeSO_4$ is used.

Question.14. What is the formula of sodium nitroprusside?
Answer. $Na_2[Fe(CN)_5NO]$.

Question.15. Why do we get violet color in the test for sulphur?
Answer. Due to the formation of $Na_4[Fe(CN)_5NOS]$ complex.

Question.16. In the detection of bromine and iodine, why the CS_2 layer is colored and not the aqueous layer?

Answer. Because Br_2 and I_2 have covalent bonding in it and hence are more soluble in organic solvent CS_2 than in water.

Question.17. How will you test bromine or iodine in the given organic compound?

Answer. Acidify the L.E. with dil HCl. Add to it 1ml of CCl_4 and then a few drops of freshly prepared Cl_2 water and shake. Orange color in CCl_4 layer indicates Br_2 while a violet color in CCl_4 layer indicates iodine

INVESTIGATORY PROJECTS 

Test the presence of ionic contamination in different samples of contaminated water.

THEORY

Presence of organic and inorganic impurities contaminate water. Organic matter such as urea, sugars, soaps, grease and inorganic matter such as ionic salts make water impure. Industrial effluents and domestic sewage are chief causes to make water contaminated. Though the water supply we get at home is treated water but at times due to high degree of contamination in water, the permissible levels of the impurities in water are not achieved by water treatment processes. This results in health hazards and waterborne diseases.

The water supply of different parts of your city may be tested for the presence of ionic contamination as per the procedure of salt analysis discussed in unit F. Presence of $Pb^{2+}, Hg^{2+}, Ca^{2+}, Mg^{2+}, Na^+, S^{2-}, Cl^-, SO_4^{2-}$ and PO_4^{3-} etc. may be tested as per the scheme discussed in that unit. The result of various samples of water tested may be recorded.

Note: Students should be encouraged to conduct this study from time to time and report their results (if objectionable) to the authorities so that a timely action can prevent people from various diseases.

OBSERVATIONS

A sample of observation table is as follows:

Ions	Experiment	Observation	Inference
1. Pb^{2+} ions	(i) Solution + potassium chromate (ii) Solution + few drops KI	Yellow ppt. which is soluble in hot NaOH Yellow ppt.	Pb^{2+} confirmed Pb^{2+} confirmed
2. Hg^{2+} ions	(i) Solution + KI (ii) Solution + Copper turnings and allow to stand (iii) Solution + Stannous chloride solution in excess	Scarlet red ppt. Greyish white deposit on the copper turnings White ppt. turning grey.	Hg^{2+} confirmed Hg^{2+} confirmed Hg^{2+} confirmed
3. Ca^{2+} ions	(i) Solution + ammonium oxalate solution. (ii) Flame test: Make a paste of the above ppt. with conc. HCl and perform flame test.	White ppt. Brick red flame	Ca^{2+} confirmed Ca^{2+} confirmed
4. Mg^{2+} ions	Solution + NH_4OH + ammonium phosphate solution and scratch the sides of the test tube with a glass rod	A white ppt. or milkiness in the solution	Mg^{2+} confirmed

5. Na^+ ions	Solution + conc. KOH + Potassium pyroantimonate solution and scratch the sides of the test tube	A white ppt. or milkiness	Na^+ confirmed
6. K^+ ions	Solution + picric acid solution	Yellow ppt.	K^+ confirmed
7. S^{2-} ions	Solution + dil. CH_3COOH + Lead acetate	Black ppt.	S^{2-} confirmed
8. Cl ions	Solution + dil. HNO_3. Boil of gases, cool and add $AgNO_3$ solution	Curdy white ppt. soluble in NH_4OH	Cl^- confirmed
9. SO_4^{2-}	Solution + $BaCl_2$ solution	White ppt. which is insoluble in all the concentrated acids	SO_4^{2-} confirmed
10. PO_4^{3-} ions	Solution + 2 − 3 drops of conc. HNO_3 and heat and add ammonium molybdate	Canary yellow ppt.	PO_4^{3-} confirmed

RESULT

S. No.	Water sample of locality	Following ions are found	
		Absent	Present
1.	A		
2.	B		
3.	C		

Checking the bacterial contamination in drinking water by testing sulphide ions.

THEORY/PRINCIPLE

Water contamination occurs due to the presence of organic (urea, sugar, grease, soaps) and inorganic (ionic salts) impurities as well as microorganisms. Presence of microorganisms, specifically bacteria can be detected by the presence of sulphide ions. Sulphide ions are produced when anaerobic bacteria decompose organic matter or reduce sulphates. Usually, effluents from paper mills, tanneries, domestic sewage and other chemical industries are responsible for the growth of bacteria and other microorganisms. These microorganisms are usually found in stagnant water.

Although, the water supply at our homes is already treated but due to the high degree of contamination in water, the permissible levels of the impurities in water are not achieved by water treatment processes. This results in health hazards and water-borne diseases.

MATERIAL REQUIRED

- Titrating flask: 1
- Starch solution: 50 g
- Iodine solution: 20 ml
- Distilled water: 500 ml
- Cadmium acetate: 0.025 M
- Sodium thiosulphate ($Na_2S_2O_3$) : 0.05 M
- Zinc acetate: 50 g

PROCEDURE

Collection and Fixing of Samples

Sulphides are readily oxidised, therefore care should be taken at the time of sampling to exclude air by flushing it with nitrogen or carbon dioxide. The best way is to 'fix' the sample immediately after collection. The fixing can be done by adding small volume of cadmium-zinc acetate solution.

1. Dissolve 50 g of cadmium acetate and 50 g of zinc acetate in 1.0 L of water to form cadmium-zinc acetate solution.
2. Take 20 ml of cadmium-zinc acetate solution and add 80 ml of water to obtain a total volume of about 100 ml.
3. If the collected sample is acidic in nature, then neutralizes it with little excess alkali.

Titration of Fixed Solution

1. Take 100 ml of fixed solution in a titration flask, add 20 ml of 0.025 M iodine solution and immediately add 15 ml of HCl (1 : 1) solution and mix them together by swirling the flask.
2. Titrate the excess iodine against 0.05 M $Na_2S_2O_3$ by adding starch solution as indicator towards the end point.
3. Calculate the amount of sulphide ions in the original samples from the amount of iodine used in the reaction with H_2S.

Chemical Reactions

$$I_2 + H_2S \longrightarrow 2HI + S$$

$$I_2 + 2\,Na_2S_2O_3 \longrightarrow 2I^- + Na_2S_4O_6 + 2Na^+$$

$$\underset{\text{thiosulphate}}{\underset{\text{Sodium}}{}} \qquad\qquad \underset{\text{tetrathionate}}{\underset{\text{Sodium}}{}}$$

RESULT

The water samples show the presence of S^{2-} ions and hence, the bacterial contamination.

PRECAUTIONS

- There should not be any insoluble impurity present in the water sample.
- Clean all the apparatus thoroughly.
- HCl is highly corrosive, so handle it carefully.

Investigation of the foaming capacity of different washing soaps and the effect of addition of sodium carbonate on them.

THEORY/PRINCIPLE

Soaps and detergents are substances which are used for Cleaning. Soaps are sodium or potassium salts of higher fatty acids containing long chains of 15 to 18 carbon atoms. The common examples are sodium palmitate, sodium stearate, sodium oleate, etc. When soap is dissolved in water, it forms lather or foam. Lather carries away dirt and grease by forming emulsion when excess of water is added.

The Cleansing action of a soap depends upon its foaming capacity, i.e., extent to which it forms lather. The foaming capacity of a soap can be compared by comparing the time taken for disappearance of foam produced in various soap solutions of same concentration. Lesser is the time taken for the foam to disappear, lower will be the foaming capacity.

Soaps have a serious limitation that they cannot be used in hard water. Hard water contains certain metal ions as Ca^{2+} and Mg^{2+}. These ions react with soap to form a curdy white precipitate called scum.

For example,

$$2C_{17}H_{35}COONa + Ca^{2+} \longrightarrow (C_{17}H_{35}COO)_2Ca + 2Na^+$$
$$2C_{17}H_{35}COONa + Mg^{2+} \longrightarrow (C_{17}H_{35}COO)_2Mg + 2Na^+$$

Soap   Magnesium   White ppt.
ions from   (scum)
hard water   Magnesium stearate

Scum, so formed, sticks to the Clothing and blocks the ability of soaps to remove oil and grease from the fabric. Therefore, it interferes with the cleaning capacity of the soap and makes the cleaning process difficult. In order to enhance the foaming capacity of soap, these Ca^{2+} and Mg^{2+} ions should be removed with the help of Na_2CO_3.

$$Ca^{2+} + Na_2CO_3 \longrightarrow CaCO_3 + 2Na^+ \quad Mg^{2+} + Na_2CO_3 \longrightarrow MgCO_3 + 2Na^+$$

Thus, addition of sodium carbonate to the soap solution removes Ca^{2+} and Mg^{2+} ions, thereby increasing the foaming capacity of soap.

◀ **PROJECT 4** ▶

Determination of the rate of evaporation of different liquids.

THEORY/PRINCIPLE

A process in which liquid molecules get converted into gaseous molecules at any temperature below its boiling point is called evaporation. Rate of evaporation of a liquid is defined as the amount of the liquid evaporating per unit time. It basically depends upon the following factors: (per unit area).

1. **Nature of liquid** Evaporator depends upon the intermolecular forces of attraction A liquid with higher boiling point (possessing strong intermolecular forces of attraction) evaporates slower than the one with lower boiling point. Stronger the intermolecular forces of attraction, smaller is the extent of vaporization or rate of evaporation. e.g. Diethyl ether evaporates more readily than propyl alcohol.
2. **Temperature** With increase in temperature, the rate of evaporation of a liquid increase. With the increase of temperature, a greater number of particles get enough kinetic energy to escape into the vapor state, thereby increasing the rate of evaporation.

3. **Surface area** Evaporation is a surface phenomenon. During evaporation, the higher energy molecules of the liquid come to the surface and escape as vapors. Thus, larger is the surface area, greater is the chance for the molecules to escape from the liquid surface to form vapors.
4. **Velocity of air currents above the liquid surface** Flow of air current carries away the gas molecules and therefore, does not allow the gas molecules to collide and get condensed back to the liquid state. Hence, the presence of air currents increases the rate of evaporation.

In this project, we will study the relationship between the rates of evaporation of different liquids and their chemical constitution.

MATERIAL REQUIRED

Weighing tubes: 4	Balance: 1
Ethanol: As per need	Tetra chloromethane: As per need
Weight box: 1	Water: As per need
Ether: As per need	Acetone: As per need

PROCEDURE

1. Take four Clean and dry weighing tubes and mark them as A, B, C, D.
2. Weigh each weighing tube with its stopper.
3. Pour 10 ml of given liquids, ethanol, ether, tetra chloromethane, acetone in different weighing tubes. Weigh each weighing tube again and find the mass of the liquid taken in each weighing tube,
4. Remove the stoppers of the weighing tubes and keep them at room temperature for one hour. Exactly after one hour, Close the mouth of all the weighing tubes with their stoppers and weigh them one by one.

OBSERVATION

Room temperature = ... °C. Time allowed for evaporation = 3600 s.

S. No.	Liquid taken	Weight of weighing bottle + liquid		Loss in weight of liquid after evaporation, $(w_1 - w_2)$ g	Rate of evaporation $\left(\dfrac{w_1 - w_2}{3600}\right)$ g^{-1}
		Before evaporation, w_1 (g)	**After evaporation, w_2 (g)**		
1.	Ethanol			-	
2.	Ether			-	
3.	Tetra chloromethane			-	
4.	Acetone			-	

RESULT

Ether has the highest rate of evaporation. The rates of evaporation are in the order:
Ether > acetone > tetrachloromethane > ethanol.

Thus, ether has weaker intermolecular forces of attraction while ethanol has stronger intermolecular forces of attraction.

PRECAUTIONS

- The temperature and the surface area should be same for the evaporation of each liquid.
- Weighing tubes of almost same size and shape should be used.

- Use same measuring cylinder for measuring all the volumes.
- Liquid should not be split while pouring.

PROJECT 5

To study the effect of acids and bases on the tensile strength of fibers.

THEORY/PRINCIPLE

Fibers are long, thin, thread like polymers which can be woven into fabrics. These fibers possess strong intermolecular forces between the chains. These forces can be dipole-dipole interactions and hydrogen bonds, e.g., in case of polyesters, the intermolecular forces are dipole-dipole interactions while in case of polyamides (like nylon), the intermolecular forces are hydrogen bonding.

The fibers are Classified into two types on the basis of their origin:

1. **Natural fibers** These may be of plant or animal origin, e.g., cotton is of plant origin and wool is of animal origin. Animal fibers are mainly made up of proteins, while fibers of plant origin are usually made up of cellulose.
2. **Synthetic fibers** These are man-made such as terylene, nylon and rayon, etc. The use of these fibers is continuously increasing because of economic factors and availability.

Fibers differ widely in their strength, chemical composition and properties. The fiber should not break easily, durable for long time, should not be easily affected by air, water, alkalies and acid because these factors affect the tensile strength of fibers.

The quality of fibers is judged on the basis of its specific gravity, action of water, acids, alkalies and other chemicals, tendency of undergoing oxidation, etc. e.g., Vegetable fibers are generally consisted of oxygen, carbon and hydrogen atoms and are polysaccharides. Therefore, they get affected by acid (their tensile strength decreases). In contrast, animal fibers are long polypeptide chains. In the presence of alkali, they break up into fragments and gradually dissolved in it (resulting in decrease in tensile strength).

TENSILE STRENGTH

The strength of the fiber is often expressed in terms 'tensile strength'. It may be defined as the extent to which a fiber can be stretched without breaking. It is a measure of the minimum weight required just to break the thread. It may be compared by taking threads of different materials and stretching them by adding weights gradually till it breaks. The weight required to break the thread gives the tensile strength of the fiber. In the given project, we will first compare the tensile strength of different fibers and then, study the effect of acids and bases on the tensile strength of different fibers.

MATERIAL REQUIRED

- Slotted weights: As per need
- Tweezer: 1
- Weight hanger: 1
- Clamp: 1
- Clamp stand: 1
- Hook: 1
- Acid [1M and 5M of HCl]: As per need
- Base [1M and 5M of NaOH]: As per need
- Different types of fibers: As per need

PROCEDURE

1. Cut out five samples of equal length (nearly 20 cm) of fiber of each type.
2. Tie one end of any one fiber with a ring fixed on an iron stand and the other end with a hanger which carries the weights to keep the fiber gets straighten.
3. Now, start adding weights onto the weight hanger and observe the stretching of the thread. Increase the weights gradually on the weight hanger till the breaking point is reached. Note the minimum weight required to break the taken thread.
4. Repeat the steps 2 and 3 with other threads made up of different materials and compare their tensile strength.

5. Now, to study the effect of acids and alkalies on the tensile strength of fibers, dip each type of fiber in dilute HCl or dilute NaOH solution of equal strengths for equal intervals of time.
6. After a small but fixed interval of time, the fibers are removed from the solution, washed with water and dried in the sun.
7. Determine again the tensile strength of the dried fibers by repeating steps 2,3 and 4.

OBSERVATION

Length of fiber = 20 cm
Strength of the acid = 1 M HCl and 5 M HCl
Strength of the base = 1 M NaOH and 5 M NaOH

S. No.	Type of fiber	Original tensile strength [Before soaking]	Tensile strength of soaked fiber (g)			
			1 M HCl	5 M HCl	1 M HCl	5 M HCl
1.	Silk					
2.	Cotton					
3.	Wool					
4.	Nylon					

CONCLUSION

The order of increasing weights required at the breaking points of threads will be the order of increasing tensile strengths.

RESULT

1. The tensile strength of the given fibers is in the order ....
2. The tensile strength of a fiber is affected by the acid and alkali effect.
   The order of the tensile strength of soak fiber is ....

PRECAUTIONS

- All fibers should be of same length and thickness. (i.e., their effective length and thickness should be same.)
- The volume and molarity of acids and bases should be same.
- Threads should be completely dipped and dried before tying their ends to hook and hanger carrying weights.
- Take same set of weights in every experiment.
- Add small weights (1-2 g) near the breaking point.

To study the methods of purification of water.

THEORY/PRINCIPLE

Purity of water obtained from different natural sources is different. The type of contamination and impurity present depends upon the source from which water is obtained. Potable water should be free from turbidity, color, odour and bacteria. It should also be free from hardness. Thus, it is essential to treat water for the removal of these contaminants. The process of removal of impurities from water so that the water becomes fit for human consumption is called water purification. The water treatment is done on a large scale and the various steps for treatment of water for purification, are described below:

STEPS FOR TREATMENT OF WATER

1. **Screening**

   The first step in purifying surface water is to remove large debris like leaves, sticks, fish, trash, etc., by passing raw water through screen with small holes. In this process, the suspended impurities are left behind the screen and clean water is sent to treatment plant. However, groundwater does not need such screening before further purification steps. Virtually, all modern water supplies for urban communities are drawn from the surface sources and not from the underground sources. Thus, screening is an important step before treatment of water.

2. **Storage**

   River water is stored in reservoirs for few days that allows solid impurities to settle down. During storage for a long time, some bacteria decrease in number as they cannot survive due to the lack of decomposing matter in screened water.

3. **Coagulation and Sedimentation of Impurities**

   Artificially controlled sedimentation basins are used for the removal of suspended impurities which are not completely removed on storage. In these basins, artificial stimulation for the coagulation of impurities is provided through introduction of active chemicals known as coagulants. The primary aim of coagulants is to provide a nucleus for agglomeration of suspended particles and increase their specific gravity to cause more rapid coagulation to form large particles which can be easily settled down. The phenomenon of joining of small particles to form larger settle able particles is known as flocculation and the larger formed particles are called floc. The commonly used coagulant is ordinary alum or aluminum sulphate. It is one of the best and almost universally applied chemical for coagulation. Some other common coagulants are iron (III) sulphate or chloride, lime, etc. The suspended impurities settle down at the bottom of the tank. A layer of sludge is formed at the bottom of the basin (or tank) and removed from time to time.

4. **Filtration**

   When all the visible suspended particles have settled down, then, water is filtered most commonly through a sand column. A layer of activated carbon is kept above the sand which removes coloring matter and odor imparting bad taste to water. The suspended impurities are trapped in pores of sand particles or adhere to sand. Thus, the sand filter renders water free of particulate matter. The sand filter may be reused by Cleaning the trapped matter. The filter is Cleaned by **back flushing**. In this process, the water is passed through the filter in the direction opposite to the normal flow of water. The adhered particles come out with opposite flow of water making the filter ready for reuse.

5. **Disinfection**

   Filtered water still may have pathogens such as bacteria, virus and protozoans. The process of rendering water free from harmful living bacteria is known as **disinfection**. Hence, filtered water is disinfected from the pathogens by chlorine gas, ozone or UV treatment.

6. **Chlorine gas and sodium hypochlorite** are the most widely used disinfectants as they are cheap and their action is rapid. These are effective in killing bacteria but have limited effectiveness against protozoans. Both of these leave strong disinfectant residuals in the water even when water enters the distribution system. The major disadvantage of using chlorine gas or sodium hypochlorite is that they react with organic compounds in the water and form harmful

chemical by products like trihalomethanes and halo acetic acid, both of these are potential carcinogenic. Chlorine also imparts some offensive odor and taste to the water.

7. **Ozone** is used in many developed countries as it is a very strong and wide spectrum disinfectant. It is most effective against all protozoans and work well against all the other pathogens. It does not form any harmful by products. There is no bad odor or taste imparted to water. This method does not leave any residual matter in water.

8. **Ultraviolet (UV) radiation** can also be used as disinfectant. It is very effective and can destroy even viruses. The major advantage of UV radiation is that like ozone it also leaves no disinfectant residual in water. It is used in aqua-guards (water purifiers) these days.

SOME OTHER METHODS OF WATER PURIFICATION

There are some other methods for the purification of water used on small scale which removes impurities and contamination to different extent. The comparison of various methods of purification will provide an idea about obtaining water of specific purity for a specific purpose.

1. Boiling

Boiling water for 15 - 20 minutes kills many harmful microorganisms and also decomposes calcium or magnesium bicarbonates into insoluble carbonates which precipitates easily thereby, decreasing the hardness of water. Drinking boiled water save us from stomach infections.

2. Distillation

This technique involves boiling of water to produce water vapors which are then condensed to get pure water. The impurities are left behind in the boiling water. Distillation gives 99.9% pure water.

3. Water Conditioning

This method is used for reducing the effects of hard water. In this technique, water with high concentrations of hardening salts is treated with sodium carbonate (soda-ash) which precipitates out the excess salts through common-ion effect.

4. Reverse Osmosis (RO)

You have seen 'RO' systems installed in your homes or in schools to get pure water. RO treatment removes salts and colored compounds from water. It involves passing of impure water through semipermeable membrane by applying high pressure to the impure water side to obtain water free from impurities. It is also used for purifying sea water.

5. Ion Exchange

Ion exchange system uses zeolite resins to replace Ca^{2+} and Mg^{2+} ions with Na^+ ions. Some synthetic ion exchange resins can remove all the ions from water and the water obtained is completely free from ions, i.e, deionized water. It is used for research purposes.

6. Carbon Filtering

Activated charcoals have high surface area and can remove many impurities through adsorption. Household water filters have activated charcoal granules. Another type of carbon filters consists sub-micrometer solid blocks of carbon. It is highly effective and removes most of the common contaminants viz pesticides, by products of disinfection chemicals, mercury, volatile organic chemicals, etc.

7. Plumbo-Solvency Reduction

Plumbo-solvency is the dissolution of lead from a lead pipe used for water supply. The problem is more in areas with naturally acidic water. It can be reduced by the addition of small quantities of phosphate ion and increasing the pH. It results in the formation of layer of insoluble lead salts on the inner surface of the pipes, thereby decreasing the chances of dissolution of lead into water.

Electrode Ionisation

In this technique, water is passed in an electrolytic cell having two electrodes separated by ion selective membrane which allows the positive ions to separate from water towards the negative electrode and negative ions from water are selectively sent towards the positive electrode. Prior to electrode ionization, the water is usually subjected to reverse osmosis in order to remove non-ionic organic contaminants. Deionized water of high purity is obtained by this technique.

MATERIAL REQUIRED

As per your need.

PROCEDURE

1. Make different groups of students with 3 - 5 students in each group.
2. Each group must study the water treatment methods used in their houses and nearby locality. Students may also find out level of purity achieved by various techniques in use, for purification of drinking water.
3. Record your observations and discuss them with other group members and your teacher.

OBSERVATION

The various water treatment methods used in locality A are .... and in locality B are ......

PROJECT 7

To analyses the hardness of different samples of water.

THEORY/PRINCIPLE

Water is hard due to the presence of calcium, magnesium and iron ions. If present in small quantities, they are not harmful for domestic use but when present in higher concentrations, they interfere in the cleansing action of soaps and detergents. Hard water when used in tea kettles, steam press and boilers, etc. form scale due to the deposition of salts which decreases the efficiency of transferring heat, thus, energy goes waste and the life of the device also decreases. Thus, the estimation and treatment of hard water becomes important.

EFFECT OF HARD WATER ON CLEANSING ACTION OF SOAP

Soaps are sodium or potassium salts of higher fatty acids such as stearic, palmitic and oleic acid. They are effective cleansing agents so long they are soluble in water. Presence of Ca^{2+} and Mg^{2+} render soaps ineffective due to the formation of insoluble calcium or magnesium stearate (scum).

$$\underset{\text{Soap}}{2C_{17}H_{35}COONa} + \underset{\text{From hard water}}{Ca^{2+}(aq)} \quad \underset{\text{Scum}}{(C_{17}H_{35}COO)_2Ca} \downarrow + 2Na^+(aq)$$

Salts of Ca^{2+} and Mg^{2+} enter into water from the reaction between slightly acidic rain water and minerals in the soil. Ground water becomes hard as it flows through underground rocks and minerals deposit. The water of the deep wells has higher degree of hardness as compared to shallow wells because of greater interaction of water with the limestone.

Disodium salt of EDTA *i.e.*; Na_2H_2Y

In aqueous solution this disodium salt dissociates into Na^+ and H_2Y^{2-} ions. Ca^{2+} and Mg^{2+} react with this H_2Y^{2-} ions to form stable complexes in a solution. The pH of the solution should be about 10. A buffer solution containing ammonia and ammonium ions is used to maintain pH as 10. End point is detected using EBT as indicator which forms complex ions with Mg^{2+} and Ca^{2+}. EBT indicator is sky blue in solution but its complex with Mg^{2+} is wine red.

$$Mg^{2+}(aq) + \underset{\text{Sky-blue}}{EBT} \longrightarrow \underset{\text{Wine red}}{[Mg - EBT]^{2+}}$$

Thus, in the beginning of titration, when EBT is added to hard water; it combines with Mg^{2+} of hard water turning wine red in color. When the titrant H_2Y^{2-} is added; H_2Y^{2-} complexes with Mg^{2+} removing Mg^{2+} from $[Mg - EBT]^{2+}$ complex, resulting in blue color at the end point.

At the end point, Mg^{2+} must be present in the solution. Therefore, a small amount of Mg^{2+} as some salt is added to the buffer solution and an equivalent amount of Na_2H_2Y is also added so that the added Mg^{2+} ions do not affect the amount of H_2Y^{2-} used during titration.

MATERIALS REQUIRED

Conical flasks, funnel, burette, pipette, EDTA (Na_2H_2Y) − Standard solution, Buffer solution of pH = 10, EBT indicator, samples of hard water.

PROCEDURE

1. Pipette out 20ml of given sample of hard water in a conical flask. Add 1ml of buffer (pH = 10) and 2 drops of EBT indicator. The color would become wine red.

2. Titrate it with standard solution of EDTA. At the end point the wine-red color disappears and the solution will turn blue. Note down the final reading and repeat the readings till concordant readings are obtained.

3. Similarly proceed with other samples of hard water.

OBSERVATIONS

Molarity of Na_2H_2Y standard solution = 0.01M
Volume of water taken = 20ml

SAMPLE A

S. No..	Initial reading	Final reading	Volume of Na_2H_2Y used ml
1.			
2.			
3.			

concordant reading = ml
Similarly record for other water samples also.

CALCULATIONS

Let the volume of Na_2H_2Y used is x ml

$$\text{Molarity of } Na_2H_2Y \text{ used} = 0.01M$$

$$\text{Moles of } Na_2H_2Y \text{ used} = \frac{M \times V}{1000} = \frac{0.01 \times x}{1000}$$

$$\text{Moles of } Na_2H_2Y = \text{Moles of } Ca^{2+} = \frac{0.01 \times x}{1000}$$

$$\text{Mass of equivalent } CaCO_3 = \frac{0.01 \times x}{1000} \times 100g = yg$$

$$\text{Mass of } CaCO_3 \text{ per liter} = \frac{y}{20} \times 1000 = 50yg/L$$

$$\text{Hardness} = 50yg/L.$$

Similarly calculate hardness of other samples of hard water.

RESULT

The hardness of different water samples is estimated as ……………....

Compare the water-soluble polyphenol (catechin) content in various samples of tea leaves.

MATERIALS REQUIRED
Conical flask, tea leaves, beakers, hot water, oven, muslin Cloth or porous paper.

THEORY/PRINCIPLE
Catechin or polyphenols are responsible for the flavors of the tea. Tea contains about 20 - 30% water soluble polyphenols. To estimate the extent of these compounds, the tea leaves are dipped in water for equal time and the loss in the weight of tea leaves is determined.

PROCEDURE
1. Weight 5 g of each tea sample and make tea bags out of it. (You may use muslin Cloth or process paper for that).
2. Take conical flasks and put 100 ml of hot water in each one of them.
3. Put different tea samples in different conical flasks and label them.
4. Remove the bags after 10 minutes.
5. Dry them in oven and take out the dried tea leaves.
6. Reweight them.
7. Note the flavour of the tea solution obtained.

OBSERVATIONS

S. No..	Brand name of tea	Initial weight	Final weight y g	Loss in weight (5 - y) g	% Of soluble polyphenol content $= \frac{y}{20} \times 100$
1.	A	5 g			
2..	B	5 g			
3.	C	5 g			

RESULT
The tea having better flavor has more catechin content.

Experiment No. ....   Date. ....

Remarks.....................   Teacher's Signature ....

Experiment No. ....   Date. ....

Remarks......................   Teacher's Signature ....

Experiment No. ....   Date. ....

Remarks.....................   Teacher's Signature ....

Experiment No. ....   Date. ....

Remarks......................   Teacher's Signature ....

Experiment No. ....   Date. ....

Remarks......................   Teacher's Signature ....

Experiment No. ....   Date. ....

Remarks......................   Teacher's Signature ....

Experiment No. ....   Date. ....

Remarks......................   Teacher's Signature ....

Experiment No. ....   Date. ....

Remarks.....................   Teacher's Signature ....

Experiment No. ....   Date. ....

Remarks.....................   Teacher's Signature ....

Experiment No. ....   Date. ....

Remarks......................   Teacher's Signature ....

Experiment No. ....   Date. ....

Remarks....................   Teacher's Signature ....

Experiment No. ....   Date. ....

Remarks......................   Teacher's Signature ....

Experiment No. ....   Date. ....

Remarks.....................   Teacher's Signature ....

Experiment No. ....   Date. ....

Remarks......................   Teacher's Signature ....

Experiment No. ....   Date. ....

Remarks.....................   Teacher's Signature ....

Experiment No. ....   Date. ....

Remarks......................   Teacher's Signature ....

Experiment No. ....   Date. ....

Remarks......................   Teacher's Signature ....

Experiment No. ....   Date. ....

Remarks.....................   Teacher's Signature ....

Experiment No. ....   Date. ....

Remarks.....................   Teacher's Signature ....

Experiment No. ....   Date. ....

Remarks......................   Teacher's Signature ....

Experiment No. ....   Date. ....

Remarks.....................   Teacher's Signature ....

Experiment No. ....   Date. ....

Remarks......................   Teacher's Signature ....

Experiment No. ....   Date. ....

Remarks.....................   Teacher's Signature ....

Experiment No. ....   Date. ....

Remarks....................   Teacher's Signature ....

Experiment No. ....   Date. ....

Remarks......................   Teacher's Signature ....

Experiment No. ....   Date. ....

Remarks.......................   Teacher's Signature ....

Experiment No. ....   Date. ....

Remarks.....................   Teacher's Signature ....

Experiment No. ....   Date. ....

Remarks....................   Teacher's Signature ....

Experiment No. ....   Date. ....

Remarks.....................   Teacher's Signature ....

Experiment No. ....   Date. ....

Remarks.....................   Teacher's Signature ....

Experiment No. ....   Date. ....

Remarks.....................   Teacher's Signature ....

Experiment No. ....   Date. ....

Remarks.....................   Teacher's Signature ....

Experiment No. ....   Date. ....

Remarks....................   Teacher's Signature ....

Experiment No. ....   Date. ....

Remarks....................   Teacher's Signature ....

Experiment No. ....   Date. ....

Remarks......................   Teacher's Signature ....

Experiment No. ....   Date. ....

Remarks.....................   Teacher's Signature ....

Experiment No. ....   Date. ....

Remarks......................   Teacher's Signature ....

Experiment No. ....   Date. ....

Remarks.....................   Teacher's Signature ....

Experiment No. ....   Date. ....

Remarks......................   Teacher's Signature ....

Experiment No. ....   Date. ....

Remarks.....................   Teacher's Signature ....

Experiment No. ....   Date. ....

Remarks.....................   Teacher's Signature ....

Experiment No. ....   Date. ....

Remarks.....................   Teacher's Signature ....

Experiment No. ....   Date. ....

Remarks.....................   Teacher's Signature ....

www.ingramcontent.com/pod-product-compliance
Lightning Source LLC
LaVergne TN
LVHW081045210726
843510LV00014B/1035